T0144301

Hawaiian Legends of Volcanoes

Hawaiian Legends of Volcanoes

W.D. Westervelt

MINT EDITIONS

Hawaiian Legends of Volcanoes was first published in 1916.

This edition published by Mint Editions 2021.

ISBN 9781513299570 | E-ISBN 9781513223834

Published by Mint Editions®

MINT
EDITIONS

minteditionbooks.com

Publishing Director: Jennifer Newens
Design & Production: Rachel Lopez Metzger
Project Manager: Micaela Clark
Typesetting: Westchester Publishing Services

Table of Contents

Introduction

The Hawaiian Islands

O f all the noteworthy groups of islands of fire rock in the Pacific Ocean, the Hawaiian Islands are the most stupendous.

The crack in the floor of the ocean upon which they are built extends from the large island Hawaii northwesterly about two thousand miles toward Japan. The islands for the first four hundred miles are large and mountainous, but as the chain is followed toward the end; the islands quickly become mere bluffs rising out of the sea, or low coral islands which have been built on the rims of submerged volcanoes.

It is interesting to note that the oldest, the smallest, and the lowest of these islands lie nearest to Japan. One of these—Midway Island—is used as the United States mid-Pacific cable station. Properly speaking, the Hawaiian Island group should cover all the islands in this chain two thousand miles long. The mountains of the large islands rise from 3,000 to 14,000 feet above the sea-level. Between this majestic range of island mountains and the "Giants of the Rockies," along the western coast of the United States, lies a rough ocean valley abounding in hills and deep ravines with an average depth under the sea-surface of about 2,600 fathoms, or 15,600 feet.

We know very little about this valley save that its floor is covered with evidences of volcanic action. Pumice and scoriæ appear to be universally distributed on the bottom of the ocean. Red and gray, and blue and green clays abound. The disintegration of pumice is given as the chief source for the formation of this clayey matter. Sometimes the deposits are permeated with meteoric or star dust.

As the ocean depths draw near the island coasts, they grow more and more shallow and become a wonderful fairy-land into which the dreamer looks from his floating canoe. Strange branching thickets of coral lie below, sometimes fringed with moving seaweeds and exquisitely colored sea-mosses, while through the coral and moss swim the marvellously painted fish of a hundred varieties. Turning and twisting in and out of coral caves are the spotted eels or the great pink or brown anemone-headed sea-worms. Sea-urchins and star-fish crawl lazily along the valleys and the uplands of the coral reef. The surface of the sea is itself covered with ceaselessly moving waves reflecting a tropical luxuriance

Of color. From well-known localities hundreds of fishermen gather spoil for the sustenance of life for themselves and their friends.

Wonderfully restful is the dream life of the winterless seas of the coral caves, and yet even today fierce floods of boiling lava sometimes find their way over the seashore and down over the reefs, destroying the life of sea-moss and coral polyps, and surrounding shells and fish and crawling slugs or swift-moving eels with floods of turbid, boiling, death-dealing water in place of the clear waves through which they had been accustomed to journey.

Each island has its individual extinct craters, but no island has any form of hot geyser action such as characterizes the Yellowstone Park of the United States, or the region around Rotorua, New Zealand. The nearest approach to a geyser deposit such as abounds in central Mexico is found on Molokai and around the small crater Leahi (Diamond Head), near Honolulu. Leahi was evidently forced up through coral reefs and the mighty heat produced small layers of geyser-like deposits.

The islands have been built up by lava alone. This lava rapidly falls to pieces under the influence of sunlight and rain, thus permitting plants, such as giant ferns, small shrubs and grasses, to take root. These plants break up the fire-rock very rapidly and send seeds broadcast to multiply soil-making activities. Thus a lava flow in a few years becomes the foundation for a growing forest.

The fire-rock, breaking through the floor of the ocean to form the Hawaiian chain of islands, lost its power first in the far northwest and cooled and hardened from island to island until it is now making its last appearance on the largest and most southeasterly of all the group, the island known by the name Hawaii. Here is still to be found what is called the largest active crater in the world, Kilauea, and the sister crater, Mokuaweoweo, from which come the most voluminous lava flows, the latest one being in May, 1916. Kilauea is about 4,000 feet altitude, while Mokuaweoweo is nearly 10,000 feet higher and is on the summit of Mauna Loa. Professor Jaggar, the experienced volcanologist in charge of an observing station on the brink of Kilauea, accepts the theory of a gas connection between these two craters so that their activity is mutual as to foam vents, but not so close that the lower volcano affords a hydrostatic outlet to the lava in the higher crater.

In this place it is well to note a fact which makes the scientific study of the active fire-lake of living volcanoes a very valuable index of coming events. Professor Jaggar says: "It has long been known that the crust of our rocky globe rises and falls with a tide similar to that of the ocean. From direct experiment professors of Chicago University have recently proved a tidal movement in the solid earth up and down of about a foot twice each day, and varying in amount through the lunar month and the solar year. There is definitely a daily movement marked in the lava level of the fire-pit of Kilauea, and there is a marked semi-annual high level." This scientific study of active craters is still in its infancy and promises, as Professor Jaggar says, "to create a new science in which we may hope at some not distant day to predict the periods of volcanic eruptions and earthquakes."

The early Hawaiians incorporated in their legends various theories to explain these great phenomena of nature, many of which are included in this volume, especially those legends which cluster around Pele, the great goddess of fire, and Hiiaka, her sister, goddess of lightning. Other interesting legends relating to the once active but long extinct crater Haleakala, on Maui, may be found in "Legends of Maui."

PART I
LEGENDS

I

Ai Laau, the Forest Eater

When Pele came to the island Hawaii, seeking a permanent home, she found another god of fire already in possession of the territory. Ai-laau was known and feared by all the people. Ai means the "one who eats or devours." Laau means "tree" or a "forest." Ai-laau was, therefore, the fire-god devouring forests. Time and again he laid the districts of South Hawaii desolate by the lava he poured out from his fire-pits.

He was the god of the insatiable appetite, the continual eater of trees, whose path through forests was covered with black smoke fragrant with burning wood, and sometimes burdened with the smell of human flesh charred into cinders in the lava flow.

Ai-laau seemed to be destructive and was so named by the people, but his fires were a part of the forces of creation. He built up the islands for future life. The process of creation demanded volcanic activity. The flowing lava made land. The lava disintegrating made earth deposits and soil. Upon this land storms fell and through it multitudes of streams found their way to the sea. Flowing rivers came from the cloud-capped mountains. Fruitful fields and savage homes made this miniature world-building complete.

Ai-laau still poured out his fire. It spread over the fertile fields, and the natives feared him as the destroyer giving no thought to the final good.

He lived, the legends say, for a long time in a very ancient part of Kilauea, on the large island of Hawaii, now separated by a narrow ledge from the great crater and called Kilauea-iki (Little Kilauea). This seems to be the first and greatest of number of craters extending in a line from the great lake of fire in Kilauea to the seacoast many miles away. They are called "The Pit Craters" because they are not hills of lava, but a series of sunken pits going deep down into the earth, some of them still having blowholes of sputtering steam and smoke.

After a time, Ai-laau left these pit craters and went into the great crater and was said to be living there when Pele came to the seashore far below.

In one of the Pele stories is the following literal translation of the account of her taking Kilauea:

"When Pele came to the island Hawaii, she first stopped at a place called Ke-ahi-a-laka in the district of Puna. From this place she began her inland journey toward the mountains. As she passed on her way there grew within her an intense desire to go at once and see Ai-laau, the god to whom Kilauea belonged, and find a resting-place with him as the end of her journey. She came up, but Ai-laau was not in his house. Of a truth he had made himself thoroughly lost. He had vanished because he knew that this one coming toward him was Pele. He had seen her toiling down by the sea at Ke-ahi-a-laka. Trembling dread and heavy fear overpowered him. He ran away and was entirely lost. When he came to that pit she laid out the plan for her abiding home, beginning at once to dig up the foundations. She dug day and night and found that this place fulfilled all her desires. Therefore, she fastened herself tight to Hawaii for all time."

These are the words in which the legend disposes of this ancient god of volcanic fires. He disappears from Hawaiian thought and Pele from a foreign land finds a satisfactory crater in which her spirit power can always dig up everlastingly overflowing fountains of raging lava.

II

How Pele Came to Hawaii

The simplest, most beautiful legend does not mention the land from which Pele started.

In this her father was Moe-moea-au-lii, the chief who dreamed of trouble. Her mother was Haumea, or Papa, who personified mother earth. Moemoea apparently is not mentioned in any other of the legends. Haumea is frequently named as the mother of Pele, as well as the heroine of many legendary experiences.

Pele's story is that of wander-lust. She was living in a happy home in the presence of her parents, and yet for a long time she was "stirred by thoughts of far-away lands." At last she asked her father to send her away. This meant that he must provide a sea-going canoe with mat sails, sufficiently large to carry a number of persons and food for many days.

"What will you do with your little egg sister?" asked her father.

Pele caught the egg, wrapped it in her skirt to keep it warm near her body, and said that it should always be with her. Evidently in a very short time the egg was changed into a beautiful little girt who bore the name Hii-aka-i-ka-poli-o-Pele (Hiiaka-in-the-bosom-of-Pele), the youngest one of the Pele family.

After the care of the helpless one had been provided for, Pele was sent to her oldest brother, Ka-moho-alii, the king of dragons, or, as he was later known in Hawaiian mythology, "the god of sharks." He was a sea-god and would provide the great canoe for the journey. While he was getting all things ready, he asked Pele where she was going. She replied, "I am going to Bola-bola; to Kuai-he-lani; to Kane-huna-moku; then to Moku-mana-mana; then to see a queen, Kaoahi her name and Niihau her island." Apparently her journey would be first to Bola-bola in the Society Islands, then among the mysterious ancestral islands, and then to the northwest until she found Niihau, the most northerly of the Hawaiian group.

The god of sharks prepared his large canoe and put it in the care of some of their relatives, Kane-pu-a-hio-hio (Kane-the-whirlwind), Ke-au-miki (The-strong-current), and Ke-au-ka (Moving-seas).

Pele was carried from land to land by these wise boatmen until at last she landed on the island Niihau. Then she sent back the boat to her brother, the shark-god. It is said that after a time he brought all the brothers and sisters to Hawaii.

Pele was welcomed and entertained. Soon she went over to Kauai, the large, beautiful garden island of the Hawaiian group. There is a story of her appearance as a dream maiden before the king of Kauai, whose name was Lohiau, whom she married, but with whom she could not stay until she had found a place where she could build a permanent home for herself and all who belonged to her.

She had a magic digging tool, Pa-oa. When she struck this down into the earth it made a fire-pit. It was with this Pa-oa that she was to build a home for herself and Lohiau. She dug along the lowlands of Kauai, but water drowned the fires she kindled, so she went from island to island but could only dig along the beach near the sea. All her fire-pits were so near the water that they burst out in great explosions of steam and sand, and quickly died, until at last she found Kilauea on the large island of Hawaii. There she built a mighty enduring palace of fire, but her dream marriage was at an end. The little sister Hiiaka, after many adventures, married Lohiau and lived on Kauai.

Another story says that Pele was the daughter of Kane-hoa-lani and Hina. The oldest and most authoritative legends say that Kane-hoa-lani was her brother and that Hina was the creator of a flood or great tidal wave which drove Pele from place to place over the ocean. This story says that Pele had a husband, Wahioloa, who ran away from her with a sister named Pele-kumu-ka-lani, and that Pele searched the islands of the great ocean as she followed them, but never found them. At last Pele came to Hawaii and escaped the flood by finding a home in Kilauea. In this story she was said to have a son Menehune and a daughter Laka. There is very little foundation for this legend. Wahioloa was a chief, well known in the legends, of a famous family of New Zealand and other South Sea islands. Laka was his son, who cut down trees by day which were set up again at night by the fairies. The Menehunes were the fairy folk of Hawaii. The story of Pele's search for a husband has been widely accepted by foreigners but not by the early Hawaiian writers.

The most authoritative story of the coming of Pele to Hawaii was published in the *Hoku-o-ka-Pakipika* (*Star of the Pacific*), in the story of *Aukele-nui-aiku*, in 1861, and in another Hawaiian paper, *Ke Kuokoa*, in 1864, and again in 1865. Again and again the legends give Ku-waha-ilo as the father and Haumea as the mother of the Pele family. Hina, is sometimes said to be Ku-waha-ilo's sister in these legends. She

W.D. WESTERVELT

quarrelled with him because he devoured all the people. The Hawaiians as a nation, even in their traditions, have never been cannibals, although their legends give many individual instances of cannibalism. The Pele stories say that "Ku-waha-ilo was a cannibal," and "Haumea was a pali (precipice or a prominent part of the earth)."

The Hawaiians, it is safe to say, had no idea of reading nature-thoughts into these expressions, thus making them "nature-myths." They probably did not understand that Ku-waha-ilo might mean destructive earth forces, and Haumea might mean the earth itself from whom Pele, the goddess of fire, and Na-maka-o-ka-hai, the goddess of the sea, were born. It is, however, interesting to note that this is the fact in the legends, and that it was in a conflict between the two sisters that Na-maka-o-ka-hai drove Pele to the Hawaiian Islands.

A greater sorcerer married Na-maka-o-ka-hai. After a time he saw Pele and her beautiful young sister Hiiaka. He took them secretly to be his wives. This sorcerer was Au-kele-nui-a-iku. *Au* might mean "to swim," and *kele* "to glide," or "slip smoothly along." The name then might mean "the great smoothly swimming son of Iku." He could fly through the heavens, swim through the seas, or run swiftly over the earth. By magic power he conquered enemies, visited strange lands, found the fountain of the water of life, sprinkled that water over his dead brothers, brought them back to life, and did many marvellous deeds. But he could not deliver Pele and Hiiaka from the wrath of their sister. High tides and floods from the seas destroyed Pele's home and lands. Then the elder brother of Pele—Ka-moho-alii, the shark-god-called for all the family to aid Pele. Na-maka-o-ka-hai fought the whole family and defeated them. She broke down their houses and drove them into the ocean. There Ka-moho-alii provided them with the great boat Honua-i-a-kea (The great spread-out world) and carried them away to distant islands.

Na-maka-o-ka-hai went to the highest of all the mythical lands of the ancestors, Nuu-mea-lani (The raised dais of heaven). There she could look over all the seas from Ka-la-kee-nui-a-Kane to Kauai, i.e., from a legendary land in the south to the most northerly part of the Hawaiian Islands. Pele carried her Pa-oa, a magic spade. Wherever they landed she struck the earth, thus opening a crater in which volcanic fires burned. As the smoke rose to the clouds, the angry watching one rushed from Nuu-mea-lani and tried to slay the family. Again and again they escaped. Farther and farther from the home land were they driven until they struck far out into the ocean.

Na-maka-o-ka-hai went back to her lookout mountain. After a long time she saw the smoke of earth-fires far away on the island Kauai. Pele had struck her Paoa into the earth, dug a deep pit, and thrown up a large hill known to this day as the Puu-o-Pele (The hill of Pele). It seemed as if an abiding-place had been found.

But the sister came and fought Pele. There is no long account of the battle. Pele was broken and smashed and left for dead. She was not dead, but she left Kauai and went to Oahu to a place near Honolulu, to Moanalua, a beautiful suburb. There she dug a fire-pit. The earth, or rather the eruption of lava, was forced up into a hill which later bore the name Ke-alia-manu (The-bird-white-like-a-salt-bed or The-white-bird). The crater which she dug filled up with salt water and was named Ke-alia-paa-kai (The-white-bed-of-salt, or Salt Lake).

Pele was not able to strike her Paoa down into a mountain side and dig deep for the foundations of her home. She could find fire only in the lowlands near the seashore. The best place on Oahu was just back of Leahi, the ancient Hawaiian name for Diamond Head. Here she threw up a great quantity of fire-rock, but at last her fires were drowned by the water she struck below.

Thus she passed along the coast of each island, the family watching and aiding until they came to the great volcano Haleakala.[1] There Pele dug with her Paoa, and a great quantity of lava was thrown out of her fire-pit.

Na-maka-o-ka-hai saw enduring clouds day after day rising with the colors of the dark dense smoke of the underworld, and knew that her sister was still living.

Pele had gained strength and confidence, therefore she entered alone into a conflict unto death.

The battle was fought by the two sisters hand to hand. The conflict lasted for a long time along the western slope of the mountain Hale-a-ka-la. Na-maka-o-ka-hai tore the body of Pele and broke her lava bones into great pieces which lie to this day along the seacoast of the district called Kahiki-nui. The masses of broken lava are called Na-iwi-o-Pele (The bones of Pele).

Pele was thought to be dead and was sorely mourned by the remaining brothers and sisters. Na-maka-o-ka-hai went off toward Nuu-mea-lani

---

1. Hale-a-ka-la must be classed as an active volcano from evidences of prehistoric fires although long extinct, but the author gives these stories in another book, "Legends of Maui."

rejoicing in the destruction of her hated enemy. By and by she looked back over the wide seas. The high mountains of the island Hawaii, snow covered, lay in the distance. But over the side of the mountain known as Mauna Loa she saw the uhane, the spirit form of Pele in clouds of volcanic smoke tinged red from the flames of raging fire-pits below.

She passed on to Nuu-mea-lani, knowing that she could never again overcome the spirit of Pele, the goddess of fire.

The Pele family crossed the channel between the islands and went to the mountain side, for they also had seen the spirit form of Pele. They served their goddess sister, caring for her fires and pouring out the destructive rivers of lava at her commands.

As time passed they became a part of the innumerable multitude of au-makuas, or ghost-gods, of the Pit of Pele, worshipped especially by those whose lives were filled with burning anger against their fellow-men.

The acceptable offerings to Pele were fruits, flowers, garlands (or leis), pigs (especially the small black pig of tender flesh and delicate flavor), chickens, fish, and men. When a family sent a part of the dead body of one of the household, it was with the prayer that the spirit might become an au-makua, and especially an unihipili au-makua. This meant a ghost-god, powerful enough to aid the worshipper to pray other people to death.

Pele is said to have become impatient at times with her brothers and sisters. Then she would destroy their pleasure resorts in the valleys. She would send a flood of lava in her anger and burn everything up.

Earthquakes came when Pele stamped the floor of the fire-pit in anger.

Flames thrusting themselves through cracks in a breaking lava crust were the fire spears of Pele's household of au-makuas or ghost-gods.

Pele's voice was explosive when angry. Therefore it was called "pu." When the natives first heard guns fired they said that the voice of the gun was "pu." It was like the explosions of gas in volcanic eruptions, and it seemed as if the foreigners had persuaded Pele to assist them in any trouble with the natives.

III

Pele and the Owl Ghost-God

M any, many years after Pele's angry sister Na-maka-o-ka-hai had driven her from the island Kauai and after the land had many dwellers therein, a quarrel arose between two of the highest chiefs of the island. They were named Koa and Kau. It did not become an open conflict immediately, but Koa was filled with such deep hatred that he was ready to employ any means to destroy his enemy.

There was a mighty Kupua, or dragon of the Pii family, at that time on Kauai. These dragons had come, according to the legends, to the Hawaiian Islands from the far-away lands of Kuai-he-lani, as attendants on the first young chief Kahanai-a-ke-Akua (The-boy-brought-up-by-the-gods). These dragons had the *mana*, or magic power of appearing as men or as dragons according to their desire.

This dragon was named Pii-ka-lalau, or Pii, the one dwelling at Ka-lalau. He was supposed to be semi-divine. His home was on the crest of an almost inaccessible precipice up which he would rush with incredible speed. Koa, the angry chief, came to this precipice and called Pii to come to him. There they plotted the death of Kau, the enemy. Assuming the appearance of a splendidly formed young man, Pii went down among the natives with Koa to watch for an opportunity to seize Kau.

After a time Kau was lured to go at night to a house far from his own home. As he entered the door he received a heavy blow which smashed the bones of one shoulder and laid him prostrate. A great giant leaped out, thrusting an enormous spear at him. Kau was one of the most skilful of all chiefs in what was known as "spear practice." He avoided the thrusts and leaped to his feet. He had a wooden dagger as his only weapon, but could not get near enough to the giant to use it.

Just as he was becoming too weary to move, his wife, who had followed him, hurled rocks, striking the giant's face, then seizing her husband fled with him homeward.

There followed a great battle in which Pii attacked all the warriors belonging to the wounded chief. The legends say that "this giant was twelve feet high, he had eyes as large as a man's fist, and an immense mouth full of tusks like those of a wild hog. His legs were as large as trees, and his weight was such that wherever he stepped there were great holes in the ground."

The warriors fled as this mighty giant charged upon them. Suddenly they stopped and rushed back. Their chief's wife had caught an ikoi, a heavy piece of wood fastened to a long, stout cord. This she hurled so that it twisted around him and bound his arms to his sides. Stones and spears beat upon him, but he broke the coco-fibre cords of the ikoi and again drove the warriors before him, trying to gain the house where the wounded chief Kau was lying.

There was an old prophetess who had rushed to the side of her master when he was brought to his home. She was one of the worshippers of Pele, the fire-goddess of the island Hawaii. Powerful were her prayers and incantations.

Soon out of the clear sky above the conflict appeared Pele hurling a fierce bolt of lightning at the giant. It struck the ground at his feet, almost overthrowing him. A second flash of lightning blinded and stunned him.

It was a curious element of old Hawaiian belief, but they did believe that demi-gods and supernatural beings had au-makuas, or ghost-gods, the spirits of their ancestors, to whom they prayed and offered sacrifice as if they were common people and needed ghost-gods to take care of them.

Pii, smitten by this new danger, called for Pueo, his most mighty ghost-god. Pele's fire-darts were falling upon him and he was near death. Then came Pueo flying down from the steep places of the mountain. Pueo was a great owl in which dwelt one of the most powerful of Pii's ancestors.

Pueo hovered over the head of Pii facing Pele. Whenever Pele hurled her fiery darts, the owl swiftly thrust his head from side to side, catching them in his beak, and with a shake of the head tossing them off to the ground.

Then came the warriors in a great body around the giant and his ghost-god. Thickly flew their spears and darts. Great clouds of stones were hurled, and both Pii and his owl-god were grievously wounded. Pele's flashes of lightning were coming with great rapidity.

The giant called to his au-makua to fly to the mountains, and then, suddenly changing himself into his dragon form, he dashed up the precipice toward his home.

The warriors were so surprised at the wonderful change that they forgot to fight, and only realized that this dragon was their enemy when they saw him far out of the reach of their best weapons. They could see that dragon leaping from stone to stone, and swiftly gliding up the steep precipice. He escaped to his home in the mountain recesses and nevermore troubled the chief by the sea. His employer was killed in a later battle. Pele returned to her home in the volcano Kilauea.

IV

The Hills of Pele

Na Puu O Pele

THROUGH THE FLEETING HOURS OF Tuesday, January eighth, in the year nineteen hundred and seven, earthquakes were felt all over the island of Hawaii. Soon after midnight as the stars of the new day Wednesday, January ninth, looked down on the melting snows of Mauna Loa, a glorious fire-light broke out on the southern slope. This light filled the sky above the mountain and was visible from all parts of the island.

The Hawaiians said "Pele has come again." For some hours great floods of lava poured forth with extraordinary activity, quickly covering a vast area of land on the side of the mountain about four thousand feet below the summit crater. Then as the brilliant light of the sun took the place of the glow of volcanic fires, clouds of eruptive gases and smoke marked the course of the lava in its flow down the mountain side. Moreover, for nearly two days the lava found an underground channel from which it burst forth at times with explosions attended by earthquakes which shook the western coast of the island. Puffs of smoke by day and pillars of fire by night marked the course of this underground channel. Thus for nearly three days the country throbbed with excitement because of the uncertainty attending the continued action of the lava flow. Then came Friday evening and a sky flooded with an ocean of fire. The lava burst from the side of the mountain about half-way between the summit and the sea in magnificent tossing waves, a river hundreds of feet across, dashing over old lava flows, burning the ferns and trees of the forest which had grown on lava a hundred years and more of age. Down it forced its way, sometimes cooling in great stone masses, crunching and crushing against each other, sometimes a rough mass of cinders resting upon a moving bed of fire and sometimes a swiftly moving liquid stream pushing from under a cooling surface and continually pressing downward toward the sea.

Meanwhile, as this lava flow was making its descent, another branch broke away westward. A little hill of lava frozen ages before into a massive breastwork of black stone standing in the front of this flow of 1907 divided it so that this western branch took its own way to the ocean beach. Thus this mighty force of melted rock from the underworld hurled its vast mass down the mountain, piling itself over all life in its path and leaving only towering heaps of desolation to cover the earth. Between these two branches of the lava river lay stretched a tract of ancient lava several miles wide, desolate and dreary save for small clumps of trees and patches of ferns and grass.

At the end of this uncovered old lava two symmetrical mounds rise from the rugged splintered rocks. These are marked on the maps of the large island as "Na Puu o Pele" (The hills of Pele).

In the summer of 1905 two friends journeyed across the desolate country which has been made more desolate by the eruption of 1907. Wearied by the hours passed in travelling over lava sharp as broken glass these friends found a grass-covered resting-place and there waited for their fatigue to pass away. In a little while some Hawaiians drew near.

"Aloha oukou (Friendship to you)!" was the greeting to them.

"Aloha olua (Friendship to you also)!" was the reply.

"This place is deserted by almost all life. Surely one cannot expect it to add any story to Hawaiian mythology."

"Ay, there is a story which belongs to the two hills of Pele down by the sea."

That summer day, on the lava of long ago, so long ago that its date is not recorded, we heard the story of the chiefs of Kahuku and the fiery and voluptuous goddess of the volcanic forces of the Hawaiian Islands.

Kahuku, the land now under past and present lava flows, was at one time luxuriant and beautiful. The sugar-cane and taro beds were bordered by flowers and shaded by long-branching trees. Villages here and there marked the population which supported the chiefs of Kahuku.

Two of the young chiefs were splendid specimens of savage manhood. They both excelled in the sports and athletic feats which were the chief occupation of those days. Wherever a hillside was covered with grass and the ground properly sloping, holua races were carried on. Very narrow sleds (holua) with long runners were used in these races.

Maidens and young men vied with each other in mad rushes over the holua courses. Usually the body was thrown headlong on the sled as it was pushed over the brink of the little hill at the beginning of the slide. Sometimes the more courageous riders would rest on hands and knees while only the very skilful dared stand upright during the swift descent.

Pele, the goddess of fire, loved this sport and often appeared as a beautiful and athletic princess. She carried her sled with her to Kahuku to the holua hillside, and easily surpassed all the women in grace and daring.

Soon the two handsome young chiefs saw her and challenged her to race with them. For hours they sported together, the chiefs led captive by the charms of the goddess.

Jealous of each other, they strove to win Pele each to his own home. Thus the days passed by, filled with sports and pleasures.

At last the young men became suspicious of their companion, her love was so fitful and capricious, sometimes burning with a raging fire toward her friends and sometimes filled with hot anger on very slight provocation.

At last a warning came that this beautiful stranger might be the goddess Pele from the other side of the island; that her home was in Halemaumau (The continuing house) of the volcano Kilauea; her attendants the always leaping flames; the caves filled with rolling waves of fire her dwelling-rooms; that she carried the control of the fires of the underworld with her wherever she went.

The young chiefs talked together concerning their experiences and then began to draw away from their dangerous visitor.

But Pele made it difficult for them to escape from her presence. She continually called them to race with her.

At last the grass began to die. The soil became warm, and the heat intense. Slight earthquakes made themselves felt. The tides were more snappy as they cast their surf waves along the beach.

The chiefs became afraid. Pele saw it and was overcome with anger. Her appearance changed. Her hair floated out in tangled masses, touched by the breath of hot winds. Her arms and limbs shone as if enwrapped with fire. Her eyes blazed like lightning, and her breath poured forth in volumes of smoke. In great terror the chiefs rushed toward the sea.

Pele struck the ground heavily with her feet. Again and again she stamped in wrath. Earthquakes swept the lands of Kahuku. Then the awful fiery flood broke from the underworld, and swept down over Kahuku. On the crest of the falling torrent of fire rode Pele, flashing the fires of her anger in great explosions above the flood.

The chiefs tried to flee toward the north, but Pele hurled the fiercest torrents beyond them to turn them back. Then they fled toward the south, but Pele again forced them back upon their own lands.

Then they hurried down to the beach, hoping to catch one of their canoes and escape on the ocean. Quickly these young men leaped on. Swiftly came the fiery flood behind them. Pele was urging the underworld forces to their utmost speed. Shrieking like fierce, whistling winds, tearing her hair and throwing it away in bunches, Pele sped after the chiefs. The floods of lava, obeying the commands of the goddess, spread out over all the land of the chiefs so that from the mountain to the sea the luxuriant lands became desolate.

Nearer and nearer to the sea came the swift runners. It seemed as if they had found the way of escape, for the surf waves waited eagerly to welcome them, and a canoe lay near the beach.

But Pele leaped from the flowing lava and threw her burning arms around the nearest one of her former lovers. In a moment the lifeless body was thrown to one side. The lava piled itself up around it, while at the command of Pele a new gush of lava rose up like a fresh crater and swallowed up all that was left.

The other chief was petrified by fear and horror. in a moment Pele seized him and called for another outburst of lava, which rose up rapidly around them. In a few minutes the Hills of Pele were built.

Thus the lovers of Pele died and thus their tombs were made. For many years, even from ancient times, they have marked the destruction of the beautiful lands of Kahuku.

Later lava flows have turned aside to spar, the monuments of the chiefs with whom Pele played for a time, and the two hills of Pele are still seen near the shore of the ocean.

V

Pele and the Chiefs of Puna

Kumu-Kahi

According to the legends, Pele was very quickly angered. Her passions were as turbulent as the lake of fire in her crater home. Her love burned, but her anger devoured. She was not safe.

Kumu-kahi was a chief who pleased Pele. According to the legends he was tall, well built, and handsome, and a great lover of the ancient games. Apparently he had known Pele only as a beautiful young chiefess; for one day, when he was playing with the people, an old woman with fiery eyes came to him demanding a share in the sports. He ridiculed her. She was very persistent. He treated her with contempt. In a moment her anger flashed out in a great fountain of volcanic fire. She chased the chief to the sea, caught him on the beach, heaped up a great mound of broken lava over him, and poured her lava flood around him and beyond him far out into the ocean.

Thus the traditions say Cape Kumu-kahi, the southeast point of the island Hawaii, was formed. Here kings, chiefs, and priests have come for ages to build great piles of lava rock with many ceremonies. The natives call these "funeral mounds" and name them after the builders, although the persons themselves were seldom placed underneath in burial.

When Hawaiians, who had been ill, recovered, they frequently vowed to make a "journey of health." This meant that they came to the place now known as Hilo Bay. There they bathed by the beautiful little Coconut Island, fished up by the demi-god Maui. There they swam around a stone known as Moku-ola (The-island-of-life). Then they walked along the seashore day after day until they were below the volcano of Kilauea. They went up to the pit of Pele, offered sacrifices, and then followed an overland path back to Hilo. It was an ill omen if for any reason they went back by the same path. They must make the "journey of health" with the face forward. Hopoe (The dancing stone), Kapoho (The green lake), and Kumu-kahi were among the places which must be visited. They all have their Pele legends.

On the shortest path from Kumu-kahi to Kilauea is a great field of many acres of lava stumps. these, according to the best theories, were made by immense floods of lava pouring down upon large forests of living trees. Lava always cools rapidly on the surface, therefore, as the lava spread out through the forest, very soon there was a great floor of hot black stone pierced by a multitude of trees. Some of these burned very slowly. The flowing lava would easily push itself up through the small opening around a burning tree and would keep on pushing and building up a higher and higher cone of lava as the tree burned away, until the tree was destroyed. These cones rise sometimes ten to fifteen feet above the lava floor. They frequently have well-preserved masses of charcoal as their core. This is nature's method of making lava stumps. This field of hundreds of lava stumps has a different origin according to the legends,

Papa-Lau-Ahi

PAPA-LAU-AHI (THE-FIRE-LEAF-SMOTHERED-OUT) WAS A CHIEF who at one time ruled the district of Puna. He excelled in the sports of the people. It was his great delight to gather all the families together and have feasts and games. He challenged the neighboring chiefs to personal contests of many kinds and almost always was the victor.

One day the chiefs were sporting on the hillsides around a plain where a multitude of people could see and applaud. Pele heard a great noise of shouting and clapping hands and desired to see the sport. In the form of a beautiful woman she suddenly appeared on the crest of one of the hills down which Papa-lau-ahi had been coasting. Borrowing a sled from one of the chiefs she prepared to race with him. He was the more skilful and soon proved to her that she was beaten. Then followed taunts and angry words and the sudden absolute loss of all self-control on the part of Pele. She stamped on the ground and floods of lava broke out, destroying many of the chiefs as they fled in every direction.

The watching people, overcome with wonder and fear, were turned into a multitude of pillars[1] of lava, never changing, never moving through all the ages.

---

1. These are the lava stumps easily visited by any lover of the curious who journeys to Kilauea.

W.D. WESTERVELT

Papa-lau-ahi fled from his antagonist, but she rode on her fiery surf waves, urging them on faster and faster until she swept him up in the flames of fire, destroying him and all his possessions.

Ke-Lii-Kuku

ANOTHER CHIEF WAS THE ONE who was called in Hawaiian legends, Ke-lii-kuku (The-Puna-chief-who-boasted). He was proud of Puna, celebrated as it was in song and legend.

"Beautiful Puna!
Clear and beautiful,
Like a mat spread out.
Shining like sunshine
Edged by the forest of Malio."

—Ancient Chant

Ke-lii-kuku visited the island Oahu. He always boasted that nothing could be compared with Puna and its sweet-scented trees and vines.

He met a prophet of Pele, Kane-a-ka-lau, whose home was on the island Kauai. The prophet asked Ke-lii-kuku about his home land. The chief was glad of an opportunity to boast. According to the "Tales of a Venerable Savage" the chief said: "I am Ke-lii-kuku of Puna. My country is charming. Abundance is found there. Rich sandy plains are there, where everything grows wonderfully."

The prophet ridiculed him, saying: "Return to your beautiful country. You will find it desolate. Pele has made it a heap of ruins. The trees have sea. The ohia[2] and puhala[3] are on the shore. The houses of your people are burned. Your land is unproductive. You have no people. You cannot live in your country any more."

The chief was angry and yet was frightened, so he told the prophet that he would go back to his own land and see if that word were true or false. If false, he would return and kill the prophet for speaking in contempt of his beautiful land. Swiftly the oarsmen and the mat sails took the chief back to his island. As he came around the eastern side

---

2. Ohia ha or Paihi = Syzygium. Ohia-lehua = Metrosideros polymorpha sandwicense.
3. Hala or Lahala = Pandanus adoratissimus.

of Hawaii he landed and climbed to the highest point from which he could have a glimpse of his loved Puna. There in the distance it lay under heavy clouds of smoke covering all the land. When the winds lifted the clouds, rolling them away, he saw that all his fertile plain was black with lava, still burning and pouring out constantly volumes of dense smoke. The remnants of forests were also covered with clouds of smoke through which darted the flashing flames which climbed to the tops of the tallest trees.

Pele had heard the boasting chief and had shown that no land around her pit of fire was secure against her will.

Ke-lii-kuku caught a long vine, hurled it over a tree, and hung himself.

Ka-Pa-Pala

ANOTHER CHIEF BY THE NAME of Ka-pa-pala heard of Pele. He went to the edge of the crater and there found a group of beautiful women. He was welcomed by Pele. They delighted in each other. Many were the games and contests. The chief was so frequently the victor that at last he boasted that he could ride his surfboard on the waves of her lake of fire. She was angry at the thought that he dared to desecrate her sacred home. He defied her, caught his surf-board, threw it on a wave as it struck the encircling wall, then leaped on his, board and launched out on the fire-waves. It is said that, to show his contempt for the power of Pele, he even stood on his head and was carried safely for a time on the crest of the red rolling surf.

Pele became very angry as she saw him fleeing from her over the lake of fire, so she called to her fire-servants, the au-makuas, or ghost-gods, of the crater, and they hurled other fire-waves across the lake against the one the chief was riding.

These twisted and turned that wave. They broke its crest. The chief and his surf-board were tossed up in a whirlpool of fire. Then he dropped into the heart of the flame and was lost.

VI

Pele's Tree

Ohia—Lehua[1] is the native name for a tree which abounds in Puna, the region of the volcanic home of the goddess Pele. It has a continual growth of delicately shaded leaves. The young leaf, pink tinted, comes as the old leaf shading into gray falls from the tree. Flowers which are like beautiful red fringed balls are always found glorifying the varicolored foliage. Here honey-loving birds and bees find their best feeding-places.

The ohia forests grow abundantly and rapidly on lava even recently thrown out by the eruptions from Pele's lake of fire. The ohia roots seem to find food and drink, where the numerous cracks of a lava field open in every direction, and vie with the tree ferns in making life take the place of the desolation caused by the volcanic floods.

About half way between the city of Hilo and the volcano Kilauea, there stood for many, many years an old ohia tree. It was so old that it had become legendary and was known as "Ka laau o Pele" (The tree of Pele). Whenever a native came near this tree, he began to search for certain leaves or fruits which he could lay beneath the tree as an offering before he dared to try to pass beyond. These sacrifices were supposed to appease the wrath of the goddess and assure the traveller safe passage through Pele's dominions.

---

1. Metrosideros polymorpha.

VII

PELE AND KAHA-WALI

For a long, long time the Hawaiians have had the proverb "Never abuse an old woman; she might be Pele."

This saying was applied to several legends, but it belonged especially to the story of her punishment of Kaha-wali. Kaha-wali was a chief born and brought up on the island Kauai. This island was one of the first on which volcanic fires were extinct. It became "The Garden Island." It was the most luxuriant in vegetation. Its hillsides were covered with grass which afforded the very best facilities for sliding down hill.

Hee-nalu meant "surf-riding," *Heeholua* meant "sled-riding," or sliding down grassy hillsides. The sleds were usually made of hard, dark kauila[1] wood. Runners made from this wood became very smooth and highly polished. They were seven, twelve, or even eighteen feet long. They were turned up a little at the front end, where they were two to four inches apart. They were fastened together with a number of crosspieces almost the full length of the runners. At the rear end the runners were about six inches apart. There were long side-pieces almost the full length of the sled. Sometimes a narrow piece of matting was fastened over the whole length of the sled, although usually only a small piece was provided for the chest to rest upon. The person using the sled grasped the right-hand side stick with his right hand, then, running swiftly to the brow of the hill, caught the stick of the left side and, throwing himself on the sled, hurled it over the edge and down the hill, sometimes sliding one hundred to two hundred yards or more. The sled was so narrow and the difficulty of staying on it so great, that it became one of the most interesting contests in which chiefs and people delighted. Much practice was necessary before the rider could maintain his or her balance, guide the sled, and gain a velocity which would carry them far beyond any competitor. Sometimes when the holua track was worn close down to the earth, grass, rushes, and even leaves, were carefully strewn over the ground to make easy gliding for the polished runners.

---

1. Columbrina oppositifolia.

Kaha-wali excelled all the Kauai chiefs in this sport, so he determined to test his skill on the other islands. He had heard of a beautiful young chiefess on the distant island Hawaii who was a wonderful holua rider. His first great contest should be with Pele. He prepared for a long journey, and a stay of many months or even years. Some authorities have placed the time of this visit to Hawaii as about the year 1350.

Kaha-wali filled his canoes with choice sleds, mats, cloaks, calabashes, spears, in fact, all the property needed for use during the visit he had in mind. He took his wife, Kanaka-wahine, his two children, his sister Koai, his younger brother, and Ahua, one of the young chiefs who was his aikane (intimate friend), and also his necessary retainers and their baggage, and among the most cherished of all, his favorite pig, Aloi-puaa. This pig was so important that its name has been made prominent in all the Kaha-wali legends.

They journeyed from island to island. Evidently his father, O-lono-hai-laau, and others of the family came as far as the island Oahu and there remained.

Kaha-wali passed on to Hawaii and landed at Kapoho in the district of Puna. Apparently the chiefs of this part of the island made Kaha-wali welcome, for he built houses for himself and his retainers and settled down as if he belonged to the country.

The visitors from Kauai entered heartily into the sports of the people and after a time climbed some lava hills and began holua races. These hills were composed of lava, which easily turned into rich soil when subdued by alternate rain and sunshine. Grass and ferns soon clothed them with abundant verdure. Holua courses were laid out, and the chiefs had splendid sport. Crowds came to watch and applaud. Musicians, dancers, wrestlers, and boxers added to the interest.

Kaha-wali and Ahua were frequently racing with each other. After each race there were dancing and games among the people. One day while racing Kaha-wali stuck his spear, which was peculiarly broad and long, into the ground at the end of the race course, then climbed the hill which bore the name Ka-hale-o-ka-mahina (The-house-of-the-moon). Ellis, who wrote the story of the missionary tour of 1823, said that the race course was pointed out to him as Ka-holua-ana-o-Kaha-vari (The-sliding-place-of-Kaha-vari). He thus describes the hill: "It was a black frowning crater about one hundred feet high, with a deep gap in the rim on the eastern side from which the course of a current of lava could be distinctly traced."

A WOMAN OF ORDINARY APPEARANCE came to the hilltop as Kaha-wali and Ahua prepared for a race. She said: "I wish to ride. Let me take your holua." The chief replied: "What does an old woman like you want with a holua? You do not belong to my family, that I should let you take mine." Then she turned to Ahua and asked for his holua. He kindly gave it to her. Together the chief and the woman dashed to the brow of the hill, threw themselves on their holuas and went headlong down the steep course. The woman soon lost her balance. The holua rolled over and hurled her some distance down the hill. She challenged the chief to another start, and when they were on the hilltop asked him for his papa-holua. She knew that a high chief's property was very sacred and could not be used by those without rank.

Kaha-wali thought this was a common native and roughly refused her request, saying: "Are you my wife (*i.e.*, my equal in rank), that you should have my holua?" Then he ran swiftly, started his holua, and sped toward the bottom of the hill.

Anger flashed in the face of the woman, for she had been spurned and deserted. Her eyes were red like hot coals of fire. She stamped on the ground. The hill opened beneath her and a flood of lava burst forth and began to pour down into the valley, following and devastating the holua course, and spreading out over the whole plain.

Assuming her supernatural form as the goddess of fire, Pele rode down the hill on her own papa-holua on the foremost wave of the river of fire. She was no longer the common native, but was the beautiful young chiefess in her fire-body, eyes flaming and hair floating back in clouds of smoke. There she stood leaning forward to catch her antagonist, and urging her fire-waves to the swiftest possible action, Explosions of bursting lava resounded like thunder all around her. Kaha-wali leaped from his holua as it came to the foot of the hill, threw off his kihei (cloak), caught his spear, and, calling Ahua to follow, ran toward the sea,

The valley quickly filled with lava, the people were speedily swallowed up. Kaha-wali rushed past his home. Ellis says: "He saw his mother who lived at Ku-kii, saluted her by touching noses, and said, 'Aloha ino oe eia ihonei paha oe e make ai, ke ai manei Pele' (Compassion rest on you. Close here perhaps is your death. Pele comes devouring).

"Then he met his wife. The fire-torrent was near at hand. She said: 'Stay with me here, and let us die together.' He said: 'No, I go! I go!'"

So he left his wife and his children. Then he met his pet hog, Aloi-puaa, and stopped for a moment to salute it by rubbing noses. The hog was caught by Pele in a few moments and changed into a great black stone in the heart of the channel and left, as the centre of the river of fire flowed on to destroy the two fleeing chiefs.—Rocks scattered along the banks of this old channel are pointed out as the individuals and the remnants of houses destroyed by Pele.

The chiefs came to a deep chasm in the earth. They could not leap over it. Kaha-wali crossed on his spear and pulled his friend over after him. On the beach he found a canoe left by his younger brother who had just landed and hastened inland to try to save his family. Kaha-wali and Ahua leaped into the boat and pushed out into the ocean.

Pele soon stood on the beach hurling red-hot rocks at him which the natives say can still be seen lying on the bottom of the sea. Thus did Kaha-wali learn that he must not abuse an old woman, for she might be Pele.

—The story often ends with the statement that Kaha-wali joined his father on the island Oahu and there remained. Other legends say he went to Kauai and there gathered a company of the most powerful priests to return to Hawaii for the destruction of Pele and her volcanic fires.

Six of these priests, according to Mrs. Rufus Lyman, who owned the land of this adventure and whose descendants still hold the same, came to Hawaii with the defeated Kaha-wali. These were Hale-mau-mau, Ka-au-ea, Uwe-kahuna, Ka-ua-nohu-nohu, Ka-lani-ua-ula, and Ka-pu-e-uli.

They took their positions near Kilauea and challenged Pele, crying out: "Where is that strange and wonderful woman?" Ka-au-ea (The fiery current) and Uwe-kahuna (priest weeping) and Hale-mau-mau (House of ferns) were kahunas, or priests of wonderful power. They were the only ones who left their names to localities in the neighborhood of Kilauea.

Hale-mau-mau had his house of ferns for a long time upon a precipice, back of the present Volcano House. From there the Dame has been changed both in meaning and location to the lava pit, the pit of Pele, in the living lake of fire, where it is called Hale-mau-mau (the-enduring-house). Ka-au-ea was the name given to a precipice in the walls of the crater. Uwe-kahuna was a high hill on the northwestern side of the crater, overlooking the fire-pit and the region around Kilauea. These priests who were also of the rank of chiefs were all killed by Pele except Kaha-wali, who escaped to Oahu.—

VIII

Pele and Kama-Puaa

Note: The adventure of the demi-god Kama-puaa has been given in "The Legends of Old Honolulu." But because it is one of the most widely told of the Pele stories, it is repeated here.

Kama-Puaa was born on the island of Oahu, where he was known as a very powerful and destructive monster, also as a peculiarly handsome and even lovable chief. He was a kupua—a being who could appear at will as an animal or man. He usually appeared as a man, but when his brutal desires to destroy overcame him or when he wished to hide from any one he adopted the form of a hog. He had the two natures, human and brutal. He had been endowed with superhuman powers, according to the legends, and was many times called Puaa-akua (Hog-god) of Oahu.

There is a curiously marked fish with an angular body and very thick skin, which is said by the Hawaiians to sometimes utter a grunting sound. It is named the Humuhumu-nukunuku-a-puaa (The-grunting-angular-pig). It was claimed that the hog-man could change himself into this fish as easily as into a hog.

An ancient chant thus described him:

> "O Kama-puaa!
> You are the one with rising bristles.
> O Rooter! O Wallower in ponds!
> O remarkable fish of the sea!
> O Youth divine!"

Kama-puaa had a beautiful magic shell—the *leho*. This was a fairy boat in which he usually journeyed from island to island. When he landed he took this shell in his hands and it grew smaller and smaller until he could tuck it away in his loin cloth. When he sailed away alone it was just large enough to satisfy his need. If some of his household travelled with him, the canoe became the large ocean boat for the family.

Some of the legends say that as a fish Kama-puaa swam through the seas to Hawaii, but others say that he used his leho boat, visited the different islands and passed slowly to the southeastern point of Hawaii to Cape Kumu-kahi.

He crossed the rough beds of lava, left by recent eruptions. He threaded his way through forests of trees and ferns and at last stood on the hills looking down upon the lake of fire. Akani-kolea was the hill upon which he stood clearly outlined against the sky.

Here was Ka-lua-Pele (The-pit-of-Pele), the home of the goddess of fire. Here she rested among glorious fountains of fire; or, rising in sport, dashed the flaming clouds in twisted masses around the precipices guarding her palace. Here Kama-puaa looked down upon a fire-dance, wherein Pele and her sisters, wrapped in filmy gowns of bluish haze, swept back and forth over the lake of fire, the pressure of their footfalls marked by hundreds of boiling bubbles rising and bursting under their tread, until the entire surface was a restless sea covered with choppy waves of fire.

Suddenly a great cloud concealed the household, then rolled away, and all the surrounding cliffs were clearly revealed. One of the sisters looking up saw Kama-puaa and cried out: "Oh, see that fine-looking man standing on Akani-kolea. He stands as straight as a precipice. His face is bright like the moon. Perhaps if our sister frees him from her tabu he can be the husband of one of us."

The sisters looked. They heard the tum-tum-tum of a small hand-gourd drum, they saw a finely formed athletic stranger, who was dancing on the hilltop, gloriously outlined in the splendor of the morning light.

Pele scorned him and said: "That is not a man, but a hog. If I ridicule him he will be angry." Then she started the war of taunting words with which chiefs usually began a conflict. She called to him giving him all the characteristics of a hog. He was angry and boasted of his power to overcome and destroy the whole Pele family. Pele thought she could easily frighten him and drive him off, so she sent clouds of sulphur-smoke and a stream of boiling lava against him. To her surprise he brushed the clouds away, with a few words checked the eruption, and stood before them unharmed.

The sisters begged Pele to send for the handsome stranger and make him a member of their family. At last she sent her brother Kane-hoa-lani to speak to him. There were many hindrances before a thorough reconciliation took place.

For a time Pele and Kama-puaa lived together as husband and wife, in various parts of the district of Puna.—The places where they dwelt are pointed out even at this day by the natives who know the traditions.—It is said that a son was born and named Opelu-haa-lii and that the fiery life of his mother was so strenuous that he lived only a little while. Some say he became the fish "Opelu."

This marriage did not endure. Kama-puaa had too many of the habits and instincts of a hog to please Pele, and she was too quickly angry to suit the overbearing Kama-puaa. Pele was never patient even with her sisters, so with Kama-puaa she would burst into fiery rage, while taunts and bitter words were freely hurled back and forth.

A sarcastic chant has been handed down among the Hawaiians as one of the taunts hurled at Pele by Kama-puaa.

> *"Makole, Makole, akahi*
> *Hele i kai o Pikeha*
> *Heaha ke ai e aiai*
> *He lihilihi pau a ke akua."*

> *"Oh, look at that one with the sore eyes!*
> *Tell her to go to the sea of Pikeha.*
> *(To wash her eyes and cure them.)*
> *What food makes her fair as the moonlight?*
> *Even her eyebrows were shaved off by some god."*

Pele was bitterly angry and tried her best to destroy her tormentor. She stamped on the ground, the earth shook, cracks opened in the surface and sometimes clouds of smoke and steam arose around Kama-puaa. He was unterrified and matched his divine powers against hers. It was demi-god against demi-goddess. It was the goddess-of-fire of Hawaii against the hog-god of Oahu. Pele's home life was given up, the bitterness of strife swept over the black sands of the seashore.

When the earth seemed ready to open its doors and pour out mighty streams of flowing lava in the defence of Pele, Kama-puaa called for the waters of the ocean to rise up. Then flood met fire and quenched it. Pele was driven inland. Her former lover, hastening after her and striving to overcome her, followed her upward until at last amid clouds of poisonous gases she went back into her spirit home in the pit of Kilauea.

Then Kama-puaa as a god of the sea gathered the waters together in great masses and hurled then, into the fire-pit. Violent explosions followed the inrush of waters. The sides of the great crater were torn to pieces by fierce earthquakes. Masses of fire expanded the water into steam, and Pele gathered the forces of the underworld to aid in driving back Kama-puaa. The lavas rose in many lakes and fountains. Rapidly the surface was cooled and the fountains checked by the water thrown in by Kama-puaa, but just as rapidly were new openings made and new streams of fire hurled at the demi-god of Oahu. It was a mighty battle of the elements.

The legends say that the hog-man, Kama-puaa, poured water into the crater until its fires were driven back to their lowest depth and Pele was almost drowned by the flood. The cloud of the skies dropped their burden of rain. All the waters of the sea that Kama-puaa could collect were poured into the crater.

Pele sent Lono-makua, who had charge over the earth-fires. He kindled eruptions manifold, but they were overwhelmed by the vast volumes of water hurled against them by Kama-puaa.

Kama-puaa raised his voice in the great ancient chant:

> *O gods in the skies!*
> *Let the rain come, let it fall.*
> *Let Paoa (Pele's spade) be broken.*
> *Let the rain be separated from the sun.*
> *O clouds in the skies!*
> *O great clouds of Iku! black as smoke!*
> *Let the heavens fall on the earth,*
> *Let the heavens roll open for the rain,*
> *Let the storm come."*

The storm fell in torrents from black clouds gathered right over the pit. The water filled the crater, according to the Hawaiian, ku-ma-waho, *i.e.*, rising until it overflowed the walls of the crater. The fires were imprisoned and drowned the home of Pele seemed to be destroyed. There remained, however, a small park of fire hidden in the breast of Lono-makua.

Pele prayed for:

> *"The bright gods of the underworld.*
> *Shining in Wawao (Vavau) are the gods of the night.*
> *The gods thick clustered for Pele."*

Kama-puaa thought he had destroyed Pele's resources, but just as his wonderful storms had put forth their greatest efforts, Lono-makua kindled the flames of fierce eruptions once more. The gods of the underworld lent their aid to the Pele family. The new attack was more than Kama-puaa could endure. The lua-pele (pit of Pele) was full of earth-fire. Streams of lava poured out against Kama-puaa.

He changed his body into a kind of grass now known as Ku-kae-puaa, filling a large field with it. When the grass lay in the pathway of the fire, the lava was turned aside for a time; but Pele, inspired by the beginning of victory, called anew upon the gods of the underworld for strong reinforcements.

Out from the pits of Kilauea came vast masses of lava piling up against the field of grass in its pathway, and soon the grass began to burn; then Kama-puaa assumed the shape of a man, the hair or bristles on his body were singed and the smart of many burns began to cause agony. Apparently the grass represented the bristles on the front of his hog-body which were scorched and burned. The legends say that since this time hogs have had very little hair on the stomach.

Down he rushed to the sea, but the lava spread out on either side cutting off retreat along the beach. Pele followed close behind, striving to overtake him before he could reach the water. The side streams had poured into the sea and the water was rapidly heated into tossing, boiling waves. Pele threw great masses of lava at Kama-puaa, striking and churning the sea into which he leaped midst the swirling heated mass. Kama-puaa gave up the battle, and, thoroughly defeated, changed himself into a fish. To that fish he gave the tough skin which he assumed when roaming over the islands as a hog. It was thick enough to withstand the boiling waves through which he swam out into the deep sea. The Hawaiians say that this fish has always been able to make a noise like the grunting of a small hog, so it was given the name Humu-humu-nuku-nuku-a-puaa.

It was said that Kama-puaa fled to foreign lands, where he married a high chiefess and lived with his family many years.

Sometime during this adventure of Kama-puaa in the domains of Pele, the islands were divided between the two demi-gods, and an oath of divine solemnity was taken by them. They set apart a large portion of the island of Hawaii for Pele, and the eastern shore from Hilo to Kohala and all the islands northwest of Hawaii as the kingdom over which Kama-puaa might establish rulers. It is said that the oath has never been broken.

One of the long legends describes a new home brought up from ocean depths by Kama-puaa, in which he established his family and from which he visited Hawaii. It says that Pele saw him and called to him:

> *"O Kama-puaa divine,*
> *My love is for you.*
> *Return, we shall have the land together,*
> *You the upland—I the lowland.*
> *Return, O my husband,*
> *Our difficulties are at an end."*

He refused, saying that it was best for them to abide by their oath, and not take any part of what belonged to the other. Perhaps this desire for reconciliation underlies the legendary love of Pele for sacrifices of those things which would most intimately connect her with Kama-puaa.

Kama-puaa has figured to the last days of Pele worship in the sacrifices offered to the fire-goddess. The most acceptable sacrifice to Pele was supposed to be puaa (a hog). If a hog could not be secured when an offering was necessary, the priest would take the fish humu-humu-nuku-nuku-a-puaa and throw it into the pit of fire. If the hog and the fish both failed, the priest would offer any of the things into which it was said in their traditions that Kama-puaa could change himself.

IX

PELE AND THE SNOW-GODDESS

There were four maidens with white mantles in the mythology of the Hawaiians. They were all queens of beauty, full of wit and wisdom, lovers of adventure, and enemies of Pele. They were the goddesses of the snow-covered mountains. They embodied the mythical ideas of spirits carrying on eternal warfare between heat and cold, fire and frost, burning lava and stony ice. They ruled the mountains north of Kilauea and dwelt in the cloud-capped summits. They clothed themselves against the bitter cold with snow-mantles. They all had the power of laying aside the white garment and taking in its place clothes made from the golden sunshine. Their stories are nature-myths derived from the power of snow and cold to check volcanic action and sometimes clothe the mountain tops and upper slopes with white, which melted as the maidens came down closer to the sea through lands made fertile by flowing streams and blessed sunshine.

It is easy to see how the story arose of Pele and Poliahu, the snow-goddess of Mauna Kea, but it is not easy to understand the different forms which the legend takes while the legends concerning the other three maidens of the white mantle are very obscure indeed.

Lilinoe was sometimes known as the goddess of the mountain Haleakala. In her hands lay the power to hold in check the eruptions which might break forth through the old cinder cones in the floor of the great crater. She was the goddess of dead fires and desolation. She sometimes clothed the long summit of the mountain with a glorious garment of snow several miles in length. Some legends give her a place as the wife of the great-flood survivor, Nana-Nuu, recorded by Fornander as having a cave-dwelling on the slope of Mauna Kea. Therefore she is also known as one of the goddesses of Mauna Kea.

Waiau was another snow-maiden of Mauna Kea, whose record in the legends has been almost entirely forgotten. There is a beautiful lake glistening in one of the crater-cones on the summit of the mountain. This was sometimes called "The Bottomless Lake," and was supposed to go down deep into the heart of the mountain. It is really forty feet in its greatest depth—deep enough for the bath of the goddess. The name Wai-au means water of sufficient depth to bathe.

Somewhere, buried in the memory of some old Hawaiian, is a legend worth exhuming, probably connecting Waiau, the maiden, with Waiau, the lake.

Kahoupokane was possibly the goddess of the mountain Hualalai, controlling the snows which after long intervals fall on its desolate summits. At present but little more than the name is known about this maiden of the snow-garment.

Poliahu, the best-known among the maidens of the mountains, loved the eastern cliffs of the great island Hawaii,—the precipices which rise from the raging surf which beats against the coast known now as the Hamakua district. Here she sported among mortals, meeting the chiefs in their many and curious games of chance and skill. Sometimes she wore a mantle of pure white kapa and rested on the ledge of rock overhanging the torrents of water which in various places fell into the sea.

There is a legend of Kauai woven into the fairy-tale of the maiden of the mist—Laieikawai—and in this story Poliahu for a short time visits Kauai as the bride of one of the high chiefs who bore the name Aiwohikupua. The story of the betrothal and marriage suggests the cold of the snow-mantle and shows the inconstancy of human hearts.

Aiwohikupua, passing near the cliffs of Hamakua, saw a beautiful woman resting on the rocks above the sea. She beckoned with most graceful gestures for him to approach the beach. Her white mantle lay on the rocks beside her. He landed and proposed marriage, but she made a betrothal with him by the exchange of the cloaks which they were wearing. Aiwohikupua went away to Kauai, but he soon returned clad in the white cloak and wearing a beautiful helmet of red feathers. A large retinue of canoes attended him, filled with musicians and singers and his intimate companions. The three mountains belonging to the snow-goddesses were clothed with snow almost down to the seashore.

Poliahu and the three other maidens of the white robe came down to meet the guests from Kauai. Cold winds swayed their garments as they drew near to the sea. The blood of the people of Kauai chilled in their veins. Then the maidens threw off their white mantles and called for the sunshine. The snow went back to the mountain tops, and the maidens, in the beauty of their golden sun-garments, gave hearty greeting to their friends. After the days of the marriage festival Poliahu and her chief went to Kauai.

A queen of the island Maui had also a promise given by Aiwohikupua. In her anger she hastened to Kauai and in the midst of the Kauai festivities revealed herself and charged the chief with his perfidy. Poliahu turned against her husband and forsook him.

The chief's friends made reconciliation between the Maui chiefess and Aiwohikupua, but when the day of marriage came the chiefess found herself surrounded by an invisible atmosphere of awful cold. This grew more and more intense as she sought aid from the chief.

At last he called to her: "This cold is the snow mantle of Poliahu. Flee to the place of fire!" But down by the fire the sun-mantle belonging to Poliahu was thrown around her and she cried out, "He wela e, he wela!" ("The heat! Oh, the heat!") Then the chief answered, "This heat is the anger of Poliahu." So the Maui chiefess hastened away from Kauai to her own home.

Then Poliahu and her friends of the white mantle threw their cold-wave over the chief and his friends and, while they shivered and were chilled almost to the verge of death, appeared before all the people standing in their shining robes of snow, glittering in the glory of the sun; then, casting once more their cold breath upon the multitude, disappeared forever from Kauai, returning to their own home on the great mountains of the southern islands.

It may have been before or after this strange legendary courtship that the snow-maiden met Pele, the maiden of volcanic fires. Pele loved the holua-coasting—the race of sleds, long and narrow, down sloping, grassy hillsides. She usually appeared as a woman of wonderfully beautiful countenance and form-a stranger unknown to any of the different companies entering into the sport. The chiefs of the different districts of the various islands had their favorite meeting-places for any sport in which they desired to engage.

There were sheltered places where gambling reigned, or open glades where boxing and spear-throwing could best be practised, or coasts where the splendid surf made riding the waves on surf-boards a scene of intoxicating delight. There were hillsides where sled-riders had opportunity for the exercise of every atom of skill and strength.

Poliahu and her friends had come down Mauna Kea to a sloping hillside south of Hamakua. Suddenly in their midst appeared a stranger of surpassing beauty. Poliahu welcomed her and the races were continued. Some of the legend-tellers think that Pele was angered by the superiority, real or fancied, of Poliahu. The ground began to grow warm and Poliahu knew her enemy.

Pele threw off all disguise and called for the forces of fire to burst open the doors of the subterranean caverns of Mauna Kea. Up toward the mountain she marshalled her fire-fountains. Poliahu fled toward the summit. The snow-mantle was seized by the outbursting lava and began to burn up. Poliahu grasped the robe, dragging it away and carrying it with her. Soon she regained strength and threw the mantle over the mountain.

There were earthquakes upon earthquakes, shaking the great island from sea to sea. The mountains trembled while the tossing waves of the conflict between fire and snow passed through and over them. Great rock precipices staggered and fell down the sides of the mountains. Clouds gathered over the mountain summit at the call of the snow-goddess. Each cloud was gray with frozen moisture and the snows fell deep and fast on the mountain. Farther and farther down the sides the snow-mantle unfolded until it dropped on the very fountains of fire. The lava chilled and hardened and choked the flowing, burning rivers.

Pele's servants became her enemies. The lava, becoming stone, filled up the holes out of which the red melted mass was trying to force itself. Checked and chilled, the lava streams were beaten back into the depths of Mauna Loa and Kilauea. The fire-rivers, already rushing to the sea, were narrowed and driven downward so rapidly that they leaped out from the land, becoming immediately the prey of the remorseless ocean.

Thus the ragged mass of Laupahoe-hoe formed, and the great ledge of the arch of Onomea, and the different sharp and torn lavas in the edge of the sea which mark the various eruptions of centuries past.

Poliahu in legendary battles has met Pele many times. She has kept the upper part of the mountain desolate under her mantle of snow and ice, but down toward the sea most fertile and luxuriant valleys and hillside slopes attest the gifts of the goddess to the beauty of the island and the welfare of men.

Out of Mauna Loa, Pele has stepped forth again and again, and has hurled eruptions of mighty force and great extent against the maiden of the snow-mantle, but the natives say that in this battle Pele has been and always will be defeated. Pele's kingdom has been limited to the southern half of the island Hawaii, while the snow-maidens rule the territory to the north.

X

Genealogy of the Pele Family

There were gods, goddesses, and ghost-gods in the Pele family. Almost all had their home in volcanic fires and were connected with all the various natural fire phenomena such as earthquakes, eruptions, smoke clouds, thunder, and lightning. Pele was the supreme ruler of the household.

She had a number of brothers and sisters. There were also many aumakuas, or ancestor ghost-gods, who were supposed to have been sent into the family by incantations and sacrifices. Sometimes when death came among the Hawaiians, a part of the body of the dead person would be thrown into the living volcano, Kilauea, with all ceremony. It was supposed that the spirit also went into the flame, finding there its permanent dwelling-place. This spirit became a Pele-au-makua.

Pele's brother, Ka-moho-alii, and her older sister, Na-maka-o-ka-hai, however, belonged to the powers of the sea. Ka-moho-alii, whose name was sometimes given as Ka-moo-alii, was king of the sharks. He was a favorite of the fire-goddess Pele. Na-maka-o-ka-hai, a sea-goddess, as a result of family trouble, became Pele's most bitter enemy, fighting her with floods of water, according to the legends.

Thus the original household represented the two eternal enemies, fire and water. One set of legends says that Kane-hoa-lani was the father and Hina-alii was the mother. Kane was one of the four great gods of Polynesia,—Ku, Kane, Lono, and Kanaloa.

Kane-hoa-lani might be interpreted as "Kane, the divine companion or friend." A better rendering is "Kane, the divine fire-maker." In most of the legends and genealogies he is given a place among Pele's brothers.

There were many Hinas. The great Hina was a goddess whose stories frequently placed her in close relation to the moon.

—It seems far-fetched to give Hina a place in the Pele family. The name was evidently brought to the Hawaiian Islands from the South Seas and in process of time was grafted into the Pele myth.—

Another set of legends published in the earliest newspapers, printed in the Hawaiian language, say that Ku-waha-ilo and Haumea were the parents. Ku was the fiercest and most powerful of the four chief gods.

Haumea had another name, Papa. She was the earth. This parentage was carried out in the most diverse as well as the most ancient of the legends and seems to be worthy of acceptance. Ku-waha-ilo is in some legends called Ku-aha-ilo. In both cases the name means "Ku with the wormy mouth," or "Ku, the man-eater" (The cannibal), whose act made him ferocious and inhuman in the eyes of the Hawaiians.

Pele has long been the fire-goddess of the Hawaiians. Her home was in the great fire-pit of the volcano of Kilauea on the island of Hawaii, and all the eruptions of lava have borne her name wherever they may have appeared. Thus the word "Pele" has been used with three distinct definitions by the old Hawaiians. Pele, the fire-goddess; Pele, a volcano or a fire-pit in any land; and Pele, an eruption of lava.

King Kalakaua was very much interested in explaining the origin of some of the great Hawaiian myths and legends. He did not make any statement about the parents of the legendary family, but said that the Pele family was driven from Samoa in the eleventh century, finding a home in the southwestern part of the island Hawaii near the volcano Kilauea. There they lived until an eruption surrounded and overwhelmed them in living fire. After a time the native imagination, which always credited ghost-gods, placed this family among the most powerful au-makuas and gave them a home in the heart of the crater. From this beginning, he thought, grew the stories of the Pele family.

The trouble with Kalakaua's version is that it does not take into account the relation of Pele to various parts of Polynesia.

The early inhabitants of the region around Hilo in the southwestern part of the island Hawaii, near Kilauea, brought many names and legends from far-away Polynesian lands to Hawaii. Hilo (formerly called Hiro), meaning to "twist" or "turn," was derived from Whiro, a great Polynesian traveller and sea-robber. The stories of Maui and Puna came from other lands, so also came some of the myths of Pele.

Fornander, in "The Polynesian Race," says: "In Hawaiian, Pele is the fire-goddess who dwells in volcanoes. In Samoan, Fee is a personage with nearly similar functions. In Tahitian, Pere is a volcano."

These varieties of the name Pele, Fornander carries back also to the pre-Malay dialects of the Indian Archipelago, where pelah means "hot," belem to "burn." Then he goes back still farther to the Celtic Bel or Belen (the sun god), the Spartan Bela (the sun), and the Babylonian god Bel. It might be worth while for some student of the Atlantic Coast or Europe to find the derivation of the name Pele as applied to the explosive volcano of Martinique, and note its apparent connection with the Pacific languages.

In Raratonga is found a legend which approaches the Hawaiian stories more nearly than any other from foreign sources. There the great goddess of fire was named Mahuike, who was known throughout Polynesia as the divine guardian of fire. It was from her that Maui the demi-god was represented by many legends as procuring fire for mankind. Her daughter, also a fire-goddess, was Pere, a name identical with the Hawaiian Pele, the letters *l* and *r* being interchangeable. This Pere became angry and blew off the top of the island Fakarava. Earthquakes and explosions terrified the people. Mahuike tried to make Pere quiet down, and finally drove her away. Pere leaped into the sea and fled to Va-ihi (Hawaii).

A somewhat similar story comes in from Samoa. Mahuike, the god of fire in Samoa, drove his daughter away. This daughter passed under the ocean from Samoa to Nuuhiwa. After establishing a volcano there, the spirit of unrest came upon her and she again passed under the sea to the Hawaiian Islands, where she determined to stay forever.

In Samoa one of the fire-gods, according to some authorities, was Fe-e, a name almost the same as Pele, yet nearly all the Samoan legends describe Fe-e as a cuttlefish possessing divine power, and at enmity with fire.

Hon. S. Percy Smith, who was for a long time Minister of Native Affairs in New Zealand and now is President of the Polynesian Society for Legendary and Historical Research, writes that the full name for Pele among the New Zealand Maoris is "Para-whenua-mea, which through well-known letter changes is identical with the full Hawaiian name Pele-honua-mea."

From several continued Pele stories in newspapers in the native language, about 1865, the following sketch of the Pele family, is compiled:

The god Ku, under the name Ku-waha-ilo, was the father. Haumea was the mother. Her father was a man-eater. Her mother was a precipice (*i.e.*, belonged to the earth). Others say Ku-waha-ilo, had neither father nor mother, but dwelt in the far-off heavens. (This probably meant that he lived beyond the most distant boundary of the horizon.)

Two daughters were born. The first, Na-maka-o-ka-hai, was born from the breasts of Haumea. Pele was born from the thighs.

After this the brothers and sisters were given life by Haumea. Ka-moho-alii, the shark-god, was born from the top of the head. He was the elder brother, the caretaker of the family, always self-denying and ready to answer any call from his relatives. Kane-hekili, Kane who had the thunder, was born from the mouth. Kauwila-nui, who ruled the lightning, came from the flashing eyes of Haumea. Thus the family came from the arms, from the wrists, the palms of the hands, the fingers, the various joints, and even from the toes. A modern reader would think that Haumea as Mother Earth threw out her children in the natural outburst of earth forces, but it is extremely doubtful if the old Hawaiians had any such idea. Yet the expression that Haumea was a precipice might imply a misty feeling in that direction.

The youngest of the family, Hiiaka-in-the-bosom-of-Pele, was born an egg. After she had been carefully warmed and nourished by Pele, she became a beautiful child. When she grew into womanhood she was the bravest, the most powerful, except Pele, and the most gentle and lovable of all the sisters.

The names of the members of the household of fire are worth noting as revealing the Hawaiian recognition of the different forces of nature. Some said there were forty sisters. One list gives only four. They were almost all called "The Hiiakas." Ellis in 1823 said the name meant "cloud holder." Fornander says it means "twilight bearer." Hii conveys the idea of lifting on the hip and arm so as to make easy. Aka means usually "shadow," and pictures the long shadows of the clouds across the sky as evening comes. There is really no twilight worth mentioning in the Hawaiian Islands and Hiiaka would be better interpreted as "lifting sunset shadows," or holding up the smoke clouds while their shadows fall over the fires of the crater, conveying the idea of firelight shining up under smoke clouds as they rise from the lake of fire.

The Hiiakas were "shadow bearers." There were eight well-known sisters:

Hiiaka-kapu-ena-ena (Hiiaka-of-the-burning-tabu), known also as Hiiaka-pua-ena-ena (Hiiaka-of-the-burning-flower) and also as Hiiaka-pu-ena-ena (Hiiaka-of-the-burning-hills).

Hiiaka-wawahi-lani (Hiiaka-breaking-the-heavens-for-the-heavy-rain-to-fall).

Hiiaka-noho-lani (Hiiaka-dwelling-in-the-skies).

Hiiaka-makole-wawahi-waa (Hiiaka-the-fire-eyed-canoe-breaker).

Hiiaka-kaa-lawa-maka (Hiiaka-with-quick-glancing-eyes).

Hiiaka-ka-lei-ia (Hiiaka-encircled-by-garlands-of-smoke-clouds).

Hiiaka-i-ka-poli-o-Pele (Hiiaka-in-the-bosom-of-Pele), who was known also as the Young Hiiaka.

Some of the legends say that Kapo was one of Pele's sisters. Kapo was a vile, murderous, poison-goddess connected with the idea of "praying to death,"[1] and in the better legends is dropped out of the Pele family.

There were eleven well-known brothers:

Ka-moho-alii (The-dragon-or-shark-king).

Kane-hekili (Kane-the-thunderer).

Kane-pohaku-kaa (Kane-rolling-stones, or The-earthquake-maker).

Kane-hoa-lani (Kane-the-divine-fire-maker).

Kane-huli-honua (Kane-turning-the-earth-upside-down-in-eruptions-and-earthquakes).

Kane-kauwila-nui (Kane-who-ruled-the-great-lightning).

Kane-huli-koa (Kane-who-broke-coral-reefs).

Ka-poha-i-kahi-ola (Explosion-in-the-place-of-life, *i.e.*, fountains of bursting gas in the living fire).

Ke-ua-a-ke-po (The-rain-in-the-night, or The-rain-of-fire-more-visible-at-night).

Ke-o-ahi-kama-kaua (The-fire-thrusting-child-of-war).

Lono-makua (Lono-the-father-who-had-charge-of-the-crater-and-its-fire).

The Thunderer and the Child-of-War were said to be hunchbacks. According to the different legends Pele had four husbands, each of whom lived with her for a time. Two of these were with her in the ancient homes of the Hawaiians, Kuai-he-lani[2] and Hapakuela. These husbands were Aukele-nui-a-iku and Wahieloa. Two husbands came to her while she dwelt in Kilauea, her palace of fire in the Hawaiian Islands. One was the rough Kama-puaa, the other was Lohiau, the handsome king of Kauai.

---

1. "Pule anana." (↑) See "Home of the Ancestors," Part II., Legends of Ghosts and Ghost-Gods.

2. "Pule anana." (↑) See "Home of the Ancestors," Part II., Legends of Ghosts and Ghost-Gods.

XI

PELE'S LONG SLEEP

Pele and her family dwelt in the beauty of Puna. On a certain day there was a fine, clear atmosphere and Pele saw the splendid surf with its white crests and proposed to her sisters to go down for bathing and surf-riding.

Pele, as the high chiefess of the family, first entered the water and swam far out, then returned, standing on the brink of the curling wave, for the very crest was her surf-board which she rode with great skill. Sometimes her brother, Kamohoalii, the great shark-god, in the form of a shark would be her surf-board. Again and again she went out to the deep pit of the waves, her sisters causing the country inland to resound with their acclamation, for she rode as one born of the sea.

At last she came to the beach and, telling the sisters that the tabu on swimming was lifted, and they could enter upon their sport, went inland with her youngest sister, Hiiaka, to watch while she slept. They went to a house thatched with ti[1] leaves, a house built for the goddess.

There Pele lay down, saying to her sister Hiiaka:

"I will sleep, giving up to the shadows of the falling evening— dropping into the very depths of slumber. Very hard will be this sleep. I am jealous of it. Therefore it is tabu. This is my command to you, O my little one. Wait you without arousing me nine days and eight nights. Then call me and chant the 'Hulihia'" (a chant supposed to bring life back and revive the body).

Then Pele added: "Perhaps this sleep will be my journey to meet a man—our husband. If I shall meet my lover in my dreams the sleep will be of great value. I will sleep."

Hiiaka moved softly about the head of her sister Pele, swaying a kahili fringed and beautiful. The perfume of the hala,[2] the fragrance of Keaau, clung to the walls of the house. From that time Puna has been famous as the land fragrant with perfume of the leaves and flowers of the hala tree.

---

1. Cordyline terminalis.
2. Same as Lahala or Puhala, Pandanus adoratissimus.

Whenever Pele slept she lost the appearance which she usually assumed, of a beautiful and glorious young woman, surpassing all the other women in the islands. Sleep brought out the aged hag that she really was. Always when any worshipper saw the group of sisters and Pele asleep in their midst they saw a weary old woman lying in the fire-bed in the great crater.

While Pele was sleeping her spirit heard the sound of a hula-drum skilfully played, accompanied by a chant sung by a wonderful voice. The spirit of Pele arose from her body and listened to that voice. She thought it was the hula[3] of Laka, who was the goddess of the dance. Then she clearly heard male voices, strong and tender, and a great joy awoke within her, and she listened toward the east, but the hula was not there. Then westward, and there were the rich tones of the beaten drum and the chant. Pele's spirit cried: "The voice of love comes on the wind. I will go and meet it."

Pele then forsook Keaau and went to Hilo, but the drum was not there. She passed from place to place, led by the call of the drum and dance, following it along the palis (precipices) and over the deep ravines, through forest shadows and along rocky beaches until she came to the upper end of Hawaii. There she heard the call coming across the sea from the island Maui. Her spirit crossed the channel and listened again. The voices of the dance were louder and clearer and more beautiful.

She passed on from island to island until she came to Kauai, and there the drum-beat and the song of the dance did not die away or change, so she knew she had found the lover desired in her dream.

Pele's spirit now put on the body of strong healthful youth. Nor was there any blemish in her beauty and symmetry from head to foot. She was anointed with all the fragrant oils of Puna. Her dress was the splendid garland of the red lehua flower and maile[4] leaf and the fern from the dwelling-places of the gods. The tender vines of the deep woods veiled this queen of the crater. In glorious young womanhood she went to the halau. The dark body of a great mist enveloped her.

The drum and the voice had led her to Haena, Kauai, to the house of Lohiau, the high-born chief of that island. The house for dancing was long and was beautifully draped with mats of all kinds. It was full of chiefs engaged in the sports of that time. The common people were gathered outside the house of the chief.

---

3. see Appendix, "Hula."
4. Alyxia olivœformis.

The multitude saw a glorious young woman step out of the mist. Then they raised a great shout, praising her with strong voices. It seemed as if the queen of sunrise had summoned the beauty of the morning to rest upon her. The countenance of Pele was like the clearest and gentlest moonlight. The people made a vacant space for the passage of this wonderful strange casting themselves on the ground before her.

An ancient chant says.

> *O the passing of that beautiful woman.*
> *Silent are the voices on the plain,*
> *No medley of the birds is in the forest;*
> *There is quiet, resting in peace."*

Pele entered the long house, passed by the place of the drums, and seated herself on a resting-place of soft royal mats.

The chiefs were astonished, and after a long time asked her if she came from the far-off sunrise of foreign lands.

Pele replied, smiling, "Ka! I belong to Kauai."

Lohiau, the high chief, said: "O stranger, child of a journey, you speak in riddles. I know Kauai from harbor to clustered hills, and my eyes have never seen any woman like you."

"Ka!" said Pele, "the place where you did not stop, there I was."

But Lohiau refused her thought, and asked her to tell truly whence she had come. At last Pele acknowledged that she had come from Puna, Hawaii,—"the place beloved by the sunrise at Haehae."

The chiefs urged her to join them in a feast, but she refused, saying she had recently eaten and was satisfied, but she "was hungry for the hula—the voices and the drum."

Then Lohiau told her that her welcome was all that he could give. "For me is the island, inland, seaward, and all around Kauai. This is your place. The home you have in Puna you will think you see again in Kauai. The name of my house for you is Ha-laau-ola (Tree of Life)."

Pele replied: "The name of your house is beautiful. My home in Puna is Mauli-ola (Long Life). I will accept this house of yours."

Lohiau watched her while he partook of the feast with his chiefs, and she was resting on the couch of mats. He was thinking of her marvellous, restful beauty, as given in the ancient chant known as "Lei Mauna Loa."

Lei of Mauna Loa, beautiful to look upon.
The mountain honored by the winds.
Known by the peaceful motion.
Calm becomes the whirlwind.
Beautiful is the sun upon the plain.
Dark-leaved the trees in the midst of the hot sun
Heat rising from the face of the moist lava.
The sunrise mist lying on the grass,
Free from the care of the strong wind.
The bird returns to rest at Palaau.
He who owns the right to sleep is at Palaau.
I am alive for your love—
For you indeed."

Then Lohiau proposed to his chiefs that he should take this beautiful chiefess from Kauai as his queen, and his thought seemed good to all. Turning to Pele, he offered himself as her husband and was accepted.

Then Lohiau arose and ordered the sports to cease while they all slept. Pele and Lohiau were married and dwelt together several days, according to the custom of the ancient time.

After this time had passed Lohiau planned another great feast and a day for the hula-dance and the many sports of the people. When they came together, beautiful were the dances and sweet the voices of Lohiau and his aikane (closest friend).

Three of the women of Kauai who were known as "the guardians of Haena" had come into the halau and taken their places near Lohiau. The people greeted their coming with great applause, for they were very beautiful and were also possessed of supernatural power. Their beauty was like that of Pele save for the paleness of their skins, which had come from their power to appear in different forms, according to their pleasure. They were female mo-o, or dragons. Their human beauty was enhanced by their garments of ferns and leaves and flowers.

Pele had told Lohiau of their coming and had charged him in these words: "Remember, you have been set apart for me. Remember, and know our companionship. Therefore I place upon you my law, 'Ke kai okia' (Cut off by the sea) are you—separated from all for me."

Lohiau looked on these beautiful women. The chief of the women, Kilinoe, was the most interesting. She refused to eat while others partook of a feast before the dancing should begin, and sat watching carefully with large, bright, shining eyes the face of Lohiau, using magic power to make him pay attention to her charms. Pele did not wish these women to know her, so placed a shadow between them and her so that they looked upon her as through a mist.

—Some legends say that Pele danced the Hula of the Winds of Kauai, calling their names until strong winds blew and storms of rain beat upon the house in which the chiefs were assembled, driving the common people to their homes.—

There the chiefs took their hula-drums and sat down preparing to play for the dancers. Then up rose Kilinoe, and, taking ferns and flowers from her skirts, made fragrant wreaths wherewith to crown Lohiau and his fellow hula-drummers, expecting the chief to see her beauty and take her for his companion. But the law of Pele was upon him and he called to her for a chant before the dance should commence.

Pele threw aside her shadow garments and came out clothed in her beautiful pa-u (skirt) and fragrant with the perfumes of Puna. She said, "It is not for me to give an olioli mele (a chant) for your native dance, but I will call the guardian winds of your islands Niihau and Kauai, O Lohiau! and they will answer my call."

Then she called for the gods who came to Hawaii; the gods of her old home now known through all Polynesia; the great gods Lono and his brothers, coming in the winds of heaven. Then she called on all the noted winds of the island Niihau, stating the directions from which they came, the points of land struck when they touched the island and their gentleness or wrath, their weakness or power, and their helpfulness or destructiveness.

For a long time she chanted, calling wind after wind, and while she sang, soft breezes blew around and through the house; then came stronger winds whistling through the trees outside. As the voice of the singer rose or fell so also danced the winds in strict harmony. While she sang, the people outside the house cried out, "The sea grows rough and white, the waves are tossed by strong winds and clouds are flying, the winds are gathering the clouds and twisting the heavens."

But one of the dragon-women sitting near Lohiau said: "The noise you think is from the sea or rustling through the leaves of the trees is only the sound of the people talking outside the great building. Their murmur is like the voice of the wind."

Then Pele chanted for the return of the winds to Niihau and its small islands and the day was of the singer softened at peace as the voice toward the end of the chant. Hushed were the people and wondering were the eyes turned upon Pele by the chiefs who were seated in the great halau. Pele leaned on her couch of soft mats and rested.

Very angry was Kilinoe, the dragon-woman. Full of fire were her eyes and dark was her face with hot blood, but she only said: "You have seen Niihau. Perhaps also you know the winds of Kauai." By giving this challenge she thought she would overthrow the power of Pele over Lohiau. She did not know who Pele was, but supposed she was one of the women of high rank native to Kauai.

Pele again chanted, calling for the guardian winds of the island Kauai:

> *"O Kauai, great island of the Lehua,*
> *Island moving in the ocean,*
> *Island moving from Tahiti,*
> *Let the winds rattle the branches to Hawaii.*
> *Let them point to the eye of the son.*
> *There is the wind of Kane at sunset—*
> *The hard night-wind for Kauai."*

Then she called for kite-flying winds when the birds sport in the heavens and the surf lies quiet on incoming waves, and then she sang of the winds kolonahe, softly blowing; and the winds hunahuna, breaking into fragments; and the winds which carry the mist, the sprinkling shower, the falling rain and the severe storm; the winds which touch the mountain-tops, and those which creep along the edge of the precipices, holding on by their fingers, and those which dash over the plains and along the sea-beach, blowing the waves into mist.

Then she chanted how the caves in the seacoast were opened and the guardians of the winds lifted their calabashes and let loose evil winds, angry and destructive, to sweep over the homes of the people and tear in pieces their fruit-trees and houses. Then Pele's voice rang out while she made known the character of the beautiful dragon-women, the guardians of the caves of Haena, calling them the mocking winds of Haena.

The people did not understand, but the dragon-women knew that Pele only needed to point them out as they sat near Lohiau, to have all the chiefs cry out against them in scorn. Out of the house they rushed, fleeing back to their home in the caves.

When Pele ceased chanting, winds without number began to come near, scraping over the land. The surf on the reef was roaring. The white sand of the beach rose up. Thunder followed the rolling, rumbling tongue of branching lightning. Mist crept over the precipices. Running water poured down the face of the cliffs. Red water and white water fled seaward, and the stormy heart of the ocean rose in tumbled heaps. The people rushed to their homes. The chiefs hastened from the house of pleasure. The feast and the day of dancing were broken up. Lohiau said to Pele: "How great indeed have been your true words telling the evil of this day. Here have come the winds and destructive storms of Haena. Truly this land has had evil today."

When Pele had laid herself down on the soft mats of Puna for her long sleep she had charged her little sister, who had been carried in her bosom, to wake her if she had not returned to life before nine days were past.

The days were almost through to the last moment when Lohiau lamented the evil which his land had felt. Then as the winds died away and the last strong gust journeyed out toward the sea Pele heard Hiiaka's voice calling from the island Hawaii in the magic chant Pele had told her to use to call her back to life.

Hearing this arousing call, she bowed her head and wept. After a time she said to Lohiau:

"It is not for me to remain here in pleasure with you. I must return because of the call of my sister. Your care is to obey my law, which is upon you. Calm will take the place of the storm, the winds will be quiet, the sea will ebb peacefully, cascades will murmur on the mountain sides, and sweet flowers will be among the leaves. I will send my little sister, then come quickly to my home in Puna."

Hiiaka knew that the time had come when she must arouse her goddess sister from that deep sleep. So she commenced the incantation which Pele told her to use. It would call the wandering spirit back to its home, no matter where it might have gone. This incantation was known as "Hulihia ke au ("The current is turning"). This was a call carried by the spirit-power of the one who uttered it into far-away places to the very person for whom it was intended. The closing lines of the incantation were a personal appeal to Pele to awake.

> "E Pele e! The milky way (the i'a) turns.
> E Pele e! The night changes.
> E Pele e! The red glow is on the island.
> E Pele e! The red dawn breaks.

E Pele e! Shadows are cast by the sunlight.
E Pele e! The sound of roaring is in your crater.
E Pele e! The uhi-uha is in your crater (this means the sound of wash
of lava is in the crater).
F Pele e! Awake, arise, return."

The spirit of Pele heard the wind, Naue, passing down to the sea and soon came the call of Hiiaka over the waters. Then she bowed down her head and wept.

When Lohiau saw the tears pouring down the face of his wife he asked why in this time of gladness she wept.

For a long time she did not reply. Then she spoke of the winds with which she had danced that night-the guardians of Niihau and Kauai, a people listening to her call, under the ruler of all the winds, the great Lono, dwelling on the waters.

Then she said: "You are my husband and I am your wife, but the call has come and I cannot remain with you. I will return to my land—to the fragrant blossoms of the hala, but I will send one of my younger sisters to come after you. Before I forsook my land for Kauai I put a charge upon my young sister to call me before nine days and nights had passed. Now I hear this call and I must not abide by the great longing of your thought."

Then the queen of fire ceased speaking and began to be lost to Lohiau, who was marvelling greatly at the fading away of his loved one, As Pele disappeared peace came to him and all the land of Kauai was filled with calm and rest.

Pele's spirit passed at once to the body lying in the house thatched with ti[5] leaves in Puna.

Soon she arose and told Hiiaka to call the sisters from the sea and they would go inland.

Then they gathered around the house in which Pele had slept. Pele told them they must dance the hula of the lifted tabu, and asked them, one after the other, to dance, but they all refused until she came to Hiiaka, who had guarded her during her long sleep. Hiiaka desired to go down to the beach and bathe with a friend, Hopoe, while the others went inland.

Pele said, "You cannot go unless you first dance for the lifted tabu."

---

5. Cordyline terminalis.

Hiiaka arose and danced gloriously before the hula god and chanted while she danced—

> *"Puna dances in the wind.*
> *The forest of Keaau is shaken.*
> *Haena moves quietly.*
> *There is motion on the beach of Nanahuki.*
> *The hula-lea danced by the wife,*
> *Dancing with the sea of Nanahuki.*
> *Perhaps this is a dance of love,*
> *For the friend loved in the sleep."*

Pele rejoiced over the skill of her younger sister and was surprised by the chanted reference to the experiences at Haena. She granted permission to Hiiaka to remain by the sea with her friend Hopoe, bathing and surf-riding until a messenger should be sent to call her home to Kilauea. Then Pele and the other sisters went inland.

XII

Hopoe, the Dancing Stone

"Moving back and forth in the wind
Softly moving in the quiet breeze
Rocking by the side of the sea."

—*Ancient Hopoe Chant*

On the southeastern seacoast of the island Hawaii, near a hamlet called Keaau, is a large stone which was formerly so balanced that it could be easily moved. One of the severe earthquake shocks of the last century overthrew the stone and it now lies a great black mass of lava rock near the seashore.

This stone in the long ago was called by the natives Hopoe, because Hopoe, the graceful dancer of Puna who taught Hiiaka, the youngest sister of Pele, how to dance, was changed into this rock. The story of the jealousy and anger of Pele, which resulted in overwhelming Hopoe in a flood of lava and placing her in the form of a balanced rock to dance by the sea to the music of the eternally moving surf, is a story which must be kept on record for the lovers of Hawaiian folk-lore.

Pele had come from the islands of the South seas and had found the Hawaiian Islands as they are at the present day. After visiting all the other islands she settled in Puna, on the large island Hawaii. There she had her long sleep in which she went to the island Kauai and found her lover Lohiau, whom she promised to send for that he might come to her home in the volcano Kilauea.

Pele called her sisters one by one and told them to go to Kauai, but they feared the uncertainty of Pele's jealousy and wrath and refused to go. At last she called for Hiiaka, but she was down by the seashore with her friend Hopoe. There in a beautiful garden spot grew the fine food plants of the old Hawaiians. There were ohias[1] (apples) and the brilliant red, feathery blossoms of the lehua trees, and there grew the hala, from which sweet-scented skirts and mats were woven.

---

1. Ohia ai = Jambosa Malacrensis. Ohia Ha = Syzygium Sandwicense.

W.D. WESTERVELT

Hopoe was very graceful and knew all the dances of the ancient people. Hour after hour she taught Hiiaka the oldest hulas (dances) known among the Hawaiians until Hiiaka excelled in all beautiful motions of the human form. Hopoe taught Hiiaka how to make leis (wreaths) from the most fragrant and splendid flowers. Together they went out into the white-capped waves bathing and swimming and seeking the fish of the coral caves. Thus they learned to have great love for each other. The girl from the south seas promised to care for the Hawaiian girl whose home was in the midst of volcanic fires, and the Hawaiian gave pledge to aid and serve as best she could.

Together they were making life happy when Pele called for Hiiaka. Out from the fumes of the crater, echoing from hill to hill through Puna, rustling the leaves of the forest trees, that insistent voice came to the younger sister.

Hiiaka by her magic power quickly passed from the seashore to the volcano. Some of the native legends say that Pele had slept near the seashore where she had commenced to build a volcanic home for herself and her sisters, and that while longing for the coming of her lover Lohiau she had dug feverishly, throwing up hills and digging some of the many pit craters which are famous in the district of Puna.

At last she determined to visit Ailaau, the god residing in Kilauea, but he had fled from her and she had taken his place and found a home in the earthquake-shaken pit of molten lava, leaping fire, and overwhelming sulphur smoke. Here she felt that her burning love could wait no longer and she must send for Lohiau.

To her came Hiiaka fresh from the clear waters of the sea and covered with leis made by her friend Hopoe. For a few minutes she stood fore her sisters. Then untwisting the wreaths one by one she danced until all the household seemed to be overcome by her grace and gladness. She sent the influence of her good-will deep into the hearts of her sisters.

Pele alone looked on with scowling dissatisfied face. As soon as she could she said to Hiiaka: "Go far away; go to Kauai; get a husband for us, and bring him to Hawaii. Do not marry him. Do not even embrace him. He is tabu to you. Go forty days only—no longer for going or coming back."

Hiiaka looked upon the imperious goddess of fire and said: "That is right. I go after your husband but I lay my charge upon you: You must take care of my lehua forest and not permit it to be injured. You may eat all other places of ours, but you must not touch my own lehua grove, my delight. You will be waiting here. Anger will arise in you. You will destroy inland: you will destroy toward the sea; but you must not touch my friend—my Hopoe. You will eat Puna with our burning wrath, but you must not go near Hopoe. This is my covenant with you, O Pele."

Pele replied: "This is right; I will care for your forest and your friend. Go you for our husband." As Pele had charged Hiiaka so had Hiiaka, laid her commandment on Pele. Hiiaka, like the other sisters, knew how uncertain Pele was in all her moods and how suddenly and unexpectedly her wrath would bring destruction upon anything appearing to oppose her. Therefore she laid upon Pele the responsibility of caring for and protecting Hopoe. This was ceremonial oath-taking between the two.

Hiiaka rose to prepare for the journey, but Pele's impatience at every moment's delay was so great that she forced Hiiaka away without food or extra clothing. Hiiaka slowly went forth catching only a magic pa-u, or skirt, which had the death-dealing power of flashing lightning.

As she climbed the walls of the crater she looked down on her sisters and chanted:

> *"The traveller is ready to go for the loved one.*
> *The husband of the dream.*
> *I stand, I journey while you remain,*
> *O women with bowed heads.*
> *Oh my lehua forest-inland at Kailu,*
> *The longing traveller journeys many days*
> *For the lover of the sweet dreams.*
> *For Lohiau ipo."*

—Ancient Hiiaka Chant

When Pele heard this chant from the forgiving love of her little sister she relented somewhat and gave Hiiaka a portion of her divine power with which to wage battle against the demons and dragons and sorcerers innumerable whom she would meet in her journey, and also sent Pauopalae, the woman of supernatural power, who cared for the ferns of all kinds around the volcano, to be her companion.

As Hiiaka went up to the highlands above the volcano she looked down over Puna. Smoke from the volcano fell toward the sea, making dark the forest along the path to Keaau, where Hopoe dwelt. Hiiaka, with a heavy heart, went on her journey, fearing that this smoke might be prophetic of the wrath of the goddess of fire visited at the suggestion of some sudden jealousy or suspicion upon Hopoe and her household.

What the Hawaiians call mana, or supernatural power able to manifest itself in many ways, had come upon Hiiaka. She found this power growing within her as she overcame obstacle after obstacle in the progress of her journey. Thus Hiiaka from time to time as she passed over the mountains of the different islands was able to look back over the dearly loved land of Puna.

At last she saw the smoke, which had clouded the forests along the way to the home of her friend, grow darker and blacker and then change into the orange hues of outbreaking fire. She felt Pele's unfaithfulness and chanted:

> *"Yellow grows the smoke of Ka-lua (the crater)*
> *Turning heavily toward the sea.*
> *Turning against my aikane (bosom friend),*
> *Coming near to my loved one,*
> *Rising up—straight up*
> *And going down from the pit."*

After many days had passed and she had found Lohiau. she had another vision of Puna and saw a great eruption of lava making desolate the land. There had been many hindrances to the progress of Hiiaka and she had been slow. The waiting and impatient goddess of fire became angry with her messenger and hurled lava from the pit crater down into the forests which she had promised to protect. Hiiaka chanted:

> *"The smoke bends over Kaliu.*
> *I thought my lehuas were tabu.*
> *The birds of fire are eating them up.*
> *They are picking my lehuas*
> *Until they are gone."*

Then from that far-off island of Kauai she looked over her burning forest toward the sea and again chanted:

"O my friend of the steep ridges above Keaau,
My friend who made garlands
Of the lehua blossoms of Kaliu,
Hopoe is driven away to the sea—
The sea of Lanahiku."

Fiercer and more devouring were the lava floods hurled out over the forest so loved Hiiaka. Heavier were the earthquake shocks shaking all the country around the volcano. Then Hiiaka bowed her head and said:

Puna is shaking in the wind,
Shaking is the hala grove of Keaau,
Tumbling are Haena and Hopoe,
Moving is the land—moving is the sea."

Thus by her spirit-power she looked back to Hawaii and saw Puna devastated and the land covered by the destructive floods of lava sent out by Pele.

Hopoe was the last object of Pele's anger at her younger sister, but there was no escape. The slow torrent of lava surrounded the beach where Hopoe waited death. She placed the garlands Hiiaka had loved over her head and shoulders. She wore the finest skirt she had woven from lauhala leaves. She looked out over the death-dealing seas into which she could not flee, and then began the dance of death.

There Pele's fires caught her but did not devour her. The angry goddess of fire took away her human life and gave her goblin power. Pele changed Hopoe into a great block of lava and balanced it on the seashore. Thus Hopoe was able to dance when the winds blew or the earth shook or some human hand touched her and disturbed her delicate poise. it is said that for centuries she has been the dancing stone of Puna.

Hiiaka fulfilled her mission patiently and faithfully, bringing Lohiau even from a grave in which he had been placed back to life and at last presenting him before Pele although all along the return journey she was filled with bitterness because of the injustice of Pele in dealing death to Hopoe.

XIII

Hiiaka's Battle with Demons

Hiiaka, the youngest sister of Pele, the goddess of fire, is the central figure of many a beautiful Hawaiian myth. She was sent on a wearisome journey over all the islands to find Lohiau, the lover of Pele.

Out of the fire-pit of the volcano, Kilauea, she climbed. Through a multitude of cracks and holes, out of which poured fumes of foul gases, she threaded her way until she stood on the highest plateau of lava the volcano had been able to build.

Pele was impatient and angry at the slow progress of Hiiaka and at first ordered her to hasten alone on her journey, but as she saw her patiently climbing along the rough way, she relented and gave to her supernatural power to aid in overcoming great difficulties and a magic skirt which had the power of lightning in its folds. But she saw that this was not enough, so she called on the divine guardians of plants to come with garments and bear a burden of skirts with which to drape Hiiaka on her journey. At last the goddess of ferns, Pau-o-palae, came with a skirt of ferns which pleased Pele. It was thrown over Hiiaka, the most beautiful drapery which could be provided.

Pau-o-palae was clothed with a network of most delicate ferns. She was noted because of her magic power over all the ferns of the forest, and for her skill in using the most graceful fronds for clothing and garlands.

Pele ordered Pau-o-palae to go with Hiiaka as her kahu, or guardian servant. She was very beautiful in her fern skirt and garland, but Hiiaka was of higher birth and nobler form and was more royal in her beauty than her follower, the goddess of ferns. It was a queen of highest legendary honor with one of her most worthy attendants setting forth on a strange quest through lands abounding in dangers and adventures.

Everywhere in ancient Hawaii were eepas, kupuas, and mo-os. Eepas were the deformed inhabitants of the Hawaiian gnomeland. They were twisted and defective in mind and body. They were the deceitful, treacherous fairies, living in the most beautiful places of the forest or glen, often appearing as human beings but always having some defect in some part of the body. Kupuas were gnomes or elves of supernatural power, able to appear in some nature-form as well as like a human being. Mo-os were the dragons of Hawaiian legends. They came to the Hawaiian islands only as the legendary memories of the crocodiles and great snakes of the lands from which the first Hawaiian natives emigrated.

Throughout Polynesia the mo-o, or moko, remained for centuries in the minds of the natives of different island groups as their most dreadful enemy, living in deep pools and sluggish streams.

Hiiaka's first test of patient endurance came in a battle with the kupuas of a forest lying between the volcano and the ocean.

The land of the island Hawaii slopes down from the raging fire-pit, mile after mile, through dense tropical forests and shining lava beds, until it enfolds, in black lava shores, the ceaselessly moving waters of the bay of Hilo. In this forest dwelt Pana-ewa, a reptile-man. He was very strong and could be animal or man as he desired, and could make the change in a moment. He watched the paths through the forest, hoping to catch strangers, robbing them and sometimes devouring them. Some he permitted to pass, but for others he made much trouble, bringing fog and rain and wind until the road was lost to them.

He ruled all the evil forces of the forest above Hilo. Every wicked sprite who twisted vines to make men stumble over precipices or fall into deep lava caves was his servant. Every demon wind, every foul fiend dwelling in dangerous branches of falling trees, every wicked gnome whirling clouds of dust or fog and wrapping them around a traveller, in fact every living thing which could in any way injure a traveller was his loyal subject. He was the kupua chief of the vicious sprites and cruel elves of the forest above Hilo. Those who knew about Pana-ewa brought offerings of awa[1] to drink, taro and red fish to eat, tapa for mats, and malos, or girdles. Then the way was free from trouble.

There were two bird-brothers of Pana-ewa; very little birds, swift as a flash of lightning, giving notice of any one coming through the forest of Pana-ewa.

Hiiaka, entering the forest, threw aside her fern robes, revealing her beautiful form. Two birds flew around her and before her. One called to the other, "This is one of the women of ka lua (the pit)." The other answered, "She is not as strong as Pana-ewa; let us tell our brother."

Hiiaka heard the birds and laughed; then she chanted, and her voice rang through all the forest:

---

1. Piper methysticum.

"Pana-ewa is a great lehua island;
A forest of ohias inland.
Fallen are the red flowers of the lehua,[2]
Spoiled are the red apples of the ohia,[2]
Bald is the head of Pana-ewa;
Smoke is over the land;
The fire is burning."

—*Translated from a Hiiaka Chant*

Hiiaka hoped to make Pana-ewa angry by reminding him of seasons of destruction by lava eruptions, which left bald lava spots in the midst of the upland forest.

Pana-ewa, roused by his bird watchmen and stirred by the taunt of Hiiaka, said. "This is Hiiaka, who shall be killed by me. I will swallow her. There is no road for her to pass."

The old Hawaiians said that Pana-ewa had many bodies. He attacked Hiiaka in his fog body, Kino-ohu, and threw around her his twisting fog-arms, chilling her and choking her and blinding her. He wrapped her in the severe cold mantle of heavy mists.

Hiiaka told her friend to hold fast to her girdle while she led the way, sweeping aside the fog with her magic skirt. Then Pana-ewa took his body called the bitter rain, ua-awa, the cold freezing rain which pinches and shrivels the skill.

He called also for the strong winds to bend down trees and smite his enemy, and lie in tangled masses in her path, so the way was hard.

Hiiaka swiftly swept her lightning skirt up against the beating rain and drove it back. Again and again she struck against the fierce storm and against the destructive winds. Sometimes she was beaten back, sometimes her arms were so weary that she could scarcely move her skirt, but she hurled it over and over against the storm until she drove it deeper into the forest and gained a little time for rest and renewal of strength.

On she went into the tangled woods and the gods of the forest rose up against her. They tangled her feet with vines. They struck her with branches of trees. The forest birds in multitudes screamed around her,

---

2. One ohia tree is supposed to bear apples, another flowers only, the flowers being called lehua. There is much confusion regard to these two trees even among botanists.

dashed against her, tried to pick out her eyes and confuse her every effort. The god and his followers brought all their power and enchantments against Hiiaka. Hiiaka made an incantation against these enemies:

> Night is at Pana-ewa and bitter is the storm;
> The branches of the trees are bent down;
> Rattling are the flowers and leaves of the lehua;
> Angrily growls the god Pana-ewa,
> Stirred up inside by his wrath.
> Oh, Pana-ewa!
> I give you hurt,
> Behold, I give the hard blows of battle."

She told her friend to stay far back in the places already conquered, while she fought with a bamboo knife in one hand and her lightning skirt in the other. Harsh noises were on every hand. From each side she was beaten and sometimes almost crushed under the weight of her opponents. Many she cut down with her bamboo knife and many she struck with her lightning skirt. The two little birds flew over the battlefield and saw Hiiaka nearly dead from wounds and weariness, and their own gods of the forest lying as if asleep. They called to Pana-ewa:

"Our gods are tired from fighting, They sleep and rest."

Pana-ewa came and looked at them. He saw that they were dead without showing deep injury, and wondered how they had been killed. The birds said, "We saw her skirt moving against the gods, up and down, back and forth."

Again the hosts of that forest gathered around the young chiefess. Again she struggled bitterly against the multitude of foes, but she was very, very tired and her arms sometimes refused to lift her knife and skirt. The discouraged woman felt that the battle was going against her, so she called for Pele, the goddess of fire.

Pele heard the noise of the conflict and the voice of her sister. She called for a body of her own servants to go down and fight the powerful kupua.

The Hawaiian legends give the name Ho-ai-ku to these reinforcements. This means "standing for food" or "devourers." Lightning storms were hurled against Pana-ewa, flashing and cutting and eating all the gods of the forest.

Hiiaka in her weariness sank down among the foes she had slain.

W.D. WESTERVELT

The two little birds saw her fall and called to Pana-ewa to go and take the one he had said he would "swallow." He rushed to the place where she lay. She saw him coming and wearily arose to give battle once more.

A great thunderstorm swept down on Pana-ewa. As he had fought Hiiaka with the cold forest winds, so Pele fought him with the storms from the pit of fire. Lightning drove him down through the forest. A mighty rain filled the valleys with red water. The kupuas were swept down the river beds and out into the ocean, where Pana-ewa and the remnant of his followers were devoured by sharks.

The Ho-ai-ku, as the legends say, went down and swallowed Pana-ewa, eating him up. Thus the land above Hilo became a safe place for the common people. To this day it is known by the name Pana-ewa.

XIV

How Hiiaka Found Wahine-Omao

The story of the journey, of the youngest sister of Pele, the goddess of volcanic fires, when seeking a husband for her oldest sister, has a simple and yet exceedingly human element in the incidents which cluster around the finding of a faithful follower and friend. It is a story of two girls attracted to each other by lovable qualities. Hiiaka was a goddess with an attendant from the old Hawaiian fairyland—the Guardian of Ferns. Then there was added the human helper, Wahine-omao, or "the light-colored woman."

While Hiiaka was journeying through the lower part of the forest which she had freed from (lemons, the Guardian of Ferns said: "I hear the grunting of a pig, but cannot tell whether it is before us or on one side. Where is it—from the sea or inland?"

Hiiaka said: "This is a pig from the sea. It is the Humuhumu-nukunuku-a-puaa. It is the grunting, angular pigfish. There is also a pig from the land. There are two pigs. They are before us. They belong to a woman and are for a gift—a sacrifice to the sister goddess who is over us two. This is Wahine-omao."

They walked on through the restful shadows of the forest and soon met a beautiful woman carrying a little black pig and a striped, angular fish. Humuhumu means "grunting." Nukunuku means "cornered." Puaa means "pig." The Humuhumu-nukunuku-a-puaa was a fish with a sharp-pointed back, grunting like a pig. It was the fish into which the fabled demi-god Kama-puaa changed himself when fleeing from the destructive fires of Pele.

Hiiaka greeted the stranger, "Love to you, O Wahine-omao."

The woman replied: "It is strange that you two have my name while your eyes are unknown to me. What are your names and where do you go?"

The sister of Pele concealed their names. "I am Ku and Ka is the name of my friend. A troublesome journey is before us beyond the waters of Hilo and the kupuas (demons) dwelling there and along the hard paths over the cliffs of the seacoast even to the steady blowing winds of Kohala."

The newcomer looked longingly into the eyes of the young chiefess and said: "I have a great desire for that troublesome journey, but this pig is a sacrifice for the goddess of the crater. Shall I throw away the pig and go with you?"

Hiiaka told her to hurry on, saying: "If your purpose is strong to go with us, take your sacrifice pig to the woman of the pit. Then come quickly after us. You will find us. While you go say continually, 'O Ku! O Ka! O Ku! O Ka!' When you arrive at the pit throw the pig down into the fire and return quickly, saying, 'O Ku! O Ka!' until you find us."

The woman said: "I will surely remember your words, but you are so beautiful and have such power that I think you are Pele. Take my pig now and end my trouble." Then she started to throw herself and her offerings on the ground before Hiiaka.

Hiiaka forbade this and explained that the offering must be taken as had been vowed.

Then the woman took her sacred gifts and went up through the woods to the crater, saying over and over, "O Ku! O Ka!" all the time realizing that new activity and life were coming to her and that she was moving as swiftly as the wind. In a little while she stood on the high point above the crater called Kolea—the place where birds rested. Before her lay a great circular plain, black-walled, full of burning lava leaping up in wonderful fire-dances and boiling violently around a group of beautiful women. She called to Pele:

> *"E Pele e! Here is my sacrifice—a pig.*
> *E Pele e! Here is my gift—a pig.*
> *Here is a pig for you,*
> *O goddess of the burning stones.*
> *Life for me. Life for you.*
> *The flowers of fire wave gently.*
> *Here is your pig."*
>
> *—Amama*

The woman threw the pig and the fish over the edge into the mystic fires beneath and leaned over, looking down into the deadliness of the fire and smoke which received the sacrifice. Flaming hands leaped up, caught the gifts and drew them down under the red surface. But in a moment there was a rush upward of a fountain of lava and hurled up with it she saw the body of the little black pig tossing in the changing jets of fire.

Down it went again into the whirling, groaning fires of the underworld. Then she knew that the sacrifice had been accepted and that she was free from her vow of service to Pele. Every tabu upon her free action had been removed and she was free—free to do according to her own wish. Then she saw one of the women of the pit slowly changing into an old woman lying on a mat of fire apart from the others. It was Pele who was always growing more and more jealous and angry with Hiiaka.

Pele called from the pit of fire, "O woman! have you seen two travellers?"

When she learned that they had been seen going on their journey she charged her new worshipper to go with Hiiaka and always spy upon her movements.

Wahine-omao became angry and cried out: "When I came here I thought you were beautiful with the glory of fire resting on you. Your sisters are beautiful, but you are a harsh old woman. Your eyes are red. Your eyebrows and hair are burned. You are the woman with scorched eyelids." Then she ran from the crater, saying, "O Ku! O Ka!" Her feet seemed to be placed on a swift-moving cloud and in a few moments she was dropped by the side of Hiiaka.

The three women, Hiiaka, the powerful, Pau-o-palae, the fairy of the ferns, and Wahine-omao, the brave and beautiful young woman of the forest, went on toward Hilo. They came to a grove of ohia, or native apple, trees, and the new friend begged them to rest for a little while in this place, for it was her father's home.

Hiiaka hesitated, saying: "I am afraid that you would entangle me, O friend! Some one is waiting below whom I must see. Our journey cannot end."

"Oh," said the woman, "I intend not to stay. Stepping sideways was my thought to see my family dwelling in this house—then journey on."

They turned aside through the red-fruited tall ohia trees to a resting-place called Papa-lau-ahi, or the fire-leaf of lava spread out flat like a board. This has always been a resting-place for travellers coming across the island to Hilo Bay. There they greeted friends and rested, but Hiiaka thought lovingly of another friend, Hopoe, far dearer to her than any one else. Tears rolled down her cheeks.

Wahine-omao said, "Why do you weep, O friend?" The reply came: "Because of my friend who lives over by that sea far below us. The smoke of the fire-anger of our sister-lord is falling over toward my friend Hopoe."

Wahine-omao said: "One of our people truly lives over there. We know and love her well, but her name is Nana-huki. The name is given because when looking at you her eyes are like a cord pulling you to her."

"Yes," said Hiiaka, "that is her name, but for me she had the sweet-scented hala wreaths and the beautiful wreaths of the red blossoms of the lehua and baskets of the most delicious treasures of the sea. So my name for her is Hopoe."

The name Hopoe may mean "one encircled," as with leis, or wreaths, or as with loving arms, or possibly it might convey the idea of one set apart in a special class or company. Both thoughts might well be included in the deep love of the young goddess for a human friend.

The time came for the three women to hasten on their way. The final alohas were said. The friends rubbed noses in the old Hawaiian way and went down to Hilo.

Hiiaka looked again from the upland over to the distant seacoast and wailed:

> *My journey opens to Kauai.*
> *Loving is my thought for my aikane,*
> *My bosom friend—*
> *Hopoe—my sweet-scented hala.*
> *Far will we go;*
> *Broad is the land;*
> *Perhaps Kauai is the end."*

Thus Hiiaka sent her loving thoughts over forest and rugged lava plains to her dearest friend even while she opened her heart to another friend who served her with the utmost faithfulness and love all the rest of her eventful journey.

XV

Hiiaka Catching a Ghost

Hiiaka, the sister of Pele, and the goddess of ferns, and their new friend Wahine-omao, were hastening through the forests above the bay of Hilo. They came near a native house. Two girls were lying on a mat near the doorway. The girls saw the strangers and with hearts full of hospitality cried: "O women strangers, stop at our house and eat. Here are dried fish and the kilu-ai (a-little-calabash-full-of-poi, the native food)." It was all the food the girls-had, but they offered it gladly.

Hiiaka said: "One of us will stop and eat. Two of us will pass on. We are not hungry." The truth was that Wahine-omao of the light skin needed food like any one not possessing semi-divine powers.

So Wahine-omao stopped and ate. She saw that the girls were kupilikia (stirred-up-with-anxiety) and asked them why they were troubled.

"Our father," they said, "went to the sea to fish in the night and has not returned. We fear that he is in trouble."

Hiiaka heard the words and looked toward the sea. She saw the spirit of that man coming up from the beach with an ipu-holoholona (a-calabash-for-carrying fish-lines, etc.) in his hands.

She charged the girls to listen carefully while she told them about their father, saying: "You must not let tears fall or wailing tones come into your voices. Your father has been drowned in the sea during the dark night. The canoe filled with water. The swift-beating waters drove your father on to the reef of coral and there his body lies. The spirit was returning home, but now sees strangers and is turning aside. I will go and chase that spirit from place to place until it goes back to the place where it left its house—the body supposed to be dead. Let no one eat until my work is done."

Hiiaka looked again toward the sea. The spirit was wandering aimlessly from place to place with its calabash thrown over its shoulder. It was afraid to come near the strangers and yet did not want to go back to the body. Hiiaka hastened after the ghost and drove it toward the house where the girls were living. She checked it as it turned to either side and tried to dash away into the forest. She pushed it into the door and called the girls in. They saw the ghost as if it were the natural body. They wept and began to beseech Hiiaka to bring him back to life.

She told them she would try, but they must remember to keep the bundle of tears inside the eyes. She told them that the spirit must take her to the body and they must wait until the rainbow colors of a divine chief came over their house. Then they would know that their father was alive. But if a heavy rain should fall they would know he was not alive and need not restrain their cries.

As Hiiaka rose to pass out of the door the ghost leaped and disappeared. Hiiaka rushed out and saw the ghost run to the sea. She leaped after it and followed it to a great stone lying at the foot of a steep precipice. There the heana (dead body) was lying. It was badly torn by the rough coral and the face had been bitten by eels. Around it lay the broken pieces of the shattered canoe. Hiiaka washed the body in the sea and then turned to look for the ghost, but it was running away as if carried by a whirlwind.

Hiiaka thrust out her "strong hand of Kilauea." This meant her power as one of the divine family living in the fire of the volcano. She thrust forth this power and turned the spirit back to the place where the body was lying. She drove the ghost to the side of the body and ordered it to enter, but the ghost thought that it would be a brighter and happier life if it could be free among the blossoming trees and fragrant ferns of the forest, so tried again to slip away from the house in which it had lived.

Hiiaka slapped the ghost back against the body and told it to go in at the bottom of a foot. She slapped the feet again and again, but it was very hard to push the ghost inside. It tried to come out as fast as Hiiaka pushed it in. Then Hiiaka uttered an incantation, while she struck the feet and limbs. The incantation was a call for the gift of life from her friends of the volcano.

"O the top of Kilauea!
O the five ledges of the pit!
The taboo fire of the woman.
When the heavens shake,
When the earth cracks open (earthquakes),
Man is thrown down,
Lying on the ground.
The lightning of Kane (a great god) wakes up.
Kane of the night, going fast.
My sleep is broken up.
E ala e! Wake up!
The heaven wakes up.

The earth inland is awake.
The sea is awake.
Awake you.
Here am I"

—Amama (The prayer is done)

By the time this chant was ended Hiiaka had forced the ghost up to the hips. There was a hard struggle—the ghost trying to go back and yet yielding to the slapping and going further and further into the body.

Then Hiiaka put forth her hand and took fresh water, pouring it over the body, chanting again:

"I make you grow, O Kane!
Hiiaka is the prophet.
This work is hers.
She makes the growth.
Here is the water of life.
E ala e! Awake! Arise!
Let life return.
The taboo (of death) is over.
It is lifted, It has flown away."

—Amama

—These were ancient chants for the restoration of life.—

All this time she was slapping and pounding the spirit into the body. It had gone up as far as the chest. Then she took more fresh water and poured it over the eyes, dashing it into the face. The ghost leaped up to the mouth and eyes—choking noises were made—the eyes opened faintly and closed again, but the ghost was entirely in the body. Slowly life returned. The lips opened and breath came back.

The healing power of Hiiaka restored the places wounded by coral rocks and bitten by eels. Then she asked him how he had been overcome. He told her he had been fishing when a great kupua came in the form of a mighty wave falling upon the boat, filling it full of water.

The fisherman said that he had tried to bail the water out of his canoe, when it was hurled down into the coral caves, and he knew nothing more until the warm sun shone in his face and his eyes opened.

Hiiaka told him to stand up, and putting out her strong hand lifted him to his feet.

He stood shaking and trembling, trying to move his feet. Little by little the power of life came back and he walked slowly to his house.

Hiiaka called for the glory of a divine chief to shine around them. Among the ancient Hawaiians it was believed that the eyes of prophets could tell the very family to which a high chief belonged by the color or peculiar appearance of the light around the individual even when a long distance away. Thus the watching anxious girls and the friends of Hiiaka knew that the ghost had gone back into the body and the fisherman had been brought back to life.

XVI

Hiiaka and the Seacoast Kupuas

Kupuas were legendary monsters which could change themselves into human beings at will. They were said to have come from far-off lands with the early settlers. They had descendants who lived along the seacoast or in out-of-the-way places inland. They were always ready to destroy and often devour any strangers passing near them. Frequently they were sharks which had a shark mouth although appearing like men. This mouth was between the shoulders and was concealed by a cape thrown carefully over the back. As human beings they would mingle with their fellows and go out in the sea, bathing and surf-riding, but when they went into the water they would dive under, assume their shark form, and catch some one of the bathers. They would carry the body to some under-water cave, where it could be devoured. All other sea monsters were given human qualities—some were helpful to men and some were destructive.

Fabled monsters lived on land. Some of these were gigantic lizards, probably the legendary memory of the crocodiles of their ancient home in India. Some were the great clouds floating in the heavens. Peculiar rocks, trees, precipices, waterfalls, birds, indeed everything with or without life, might be given human and supernatural power and called kupuas. After a time various objects began to have worshippers who became priests supposed to be endowed with the qualities of the objects worshipped. These, in the later days, have been considered sorcerers or witches, receiving the name kupuas.

Makaukiu

Hiiaka, the sister of Pele, the goddess of volcanoes, by her magic power was able to find and destroy many of these mysterious monsters. She bad two companions as she journeyed along the eastern coast of the island Hawaii, Their way was frequently very wearisome as they climbed down steep precipices into valleys and gulches and then had to climb up on the other side.

In one valley beautiful clear sea-water invited the girls to bathe. Two of them threw aside their tapa clothes and ran down to the beach.

Hiiaka bade them wait, telling them this was the home of Makaukiu, a very ferocious monster. But the girls thought they could see any evil one, if living in that pure, clear water, so they laughed at their friend and went to the edge of the water. Hiiaka took some fragrant ti-leaves, made a little bundle and threw it into the sea. The girls made ready to leap and swim, when suddenly Makaukiu appeared just below the surface, catching and shaking the leaves.

The girls fled inland to higher ground, but Hiiaka stood at the edge of the sea. The sea monster tried to catch her in his great mouth. He lashed the water into foam, trying to strike her with his tail. He tried to wash her into the sea by pushing great, whirling waves against her, but Hiiaka struck him with the mighty forces of lightning and fire which she had in her magic skirt. Soon he was dead and his body floated on the water until the tide swept it out to sink in the deep sea. The place where this monster was slain was given his name and is still called "The Swimming-Hole of Makaukiu."

Mahiki

THE HAWAIIANS SAY THAT THE desire for battle was burning in the heart of Hiiaka and she longed to kill Mahiki, who lived near Waipio Valley—one of the most beautiful of all the valleys of the Hawaiian Islands. Mahiki was a whirlwind. When he saw the girls coming he fled inland, hiding himself in a cloud of dust. Whenever the girls came toward him he fled swiftly to a new place. They could not catch and destroy him.

As they were following the whirlwind they heard some one calling. They stopped and found two persons without bones—the bodies were flesh, soft and yielding, yet of human form. Hiiaka had pity on them, so she took the ribs of a long leaf and pushed them into the soft bodies, where they became bones. Then the two could stand. After a time they could use their new bones in their legs and walk.

Pili and Noho

HIIAKA REMEMBERED THAT THERE WERE two dragons in the river Wailuku, a river of swift cascades and beautiful waterfalls near Hilo, so she turned back filled with the wish to destroy them and free the people from that danger.

At the place where the people crossed the river were two things which looked like large, flat logs tossing in the water. Any person wishing to cross the river would lay fish, sweet potatoes, and other kinds of food on the logs. When these things disappeared the logs would act sometimes as a bridge and sometimes as a boat, taking those who had given presents across the river. These logs were the great tongues of the dragons Pili-a-moo and Noho-a-moo, i.e., the dragon Pili and the dragon Noho.

Hiiaka and her two companions came to the river side. The travellers called for an open way across.

One dragon said to the other, "Here comes one of our family."

The other said: "What of that? She can cross if she pays. If she does not give our price, she shall not go over in this place."

Hiiaka ordered the dragons to prepare her way, but they refused. Then she taunted them as slaves, ordering them to bring vegetable food and fish. The dragons became angry and thrashed the water into whirlpools, trying to catch the travellers and pull them into the river. The people from far and near gathered to the place of this strange conflict.

A chief laughed at Hiiaka, saying, "These are dragon-gods, and yet you dispute with them!"

Hiiaka said, "Yes, they are dragon-gods, but when I attack them they will die."

The chief offered to make any bet desired that she could not injure the dragons.

Hiiaka said, "I have no property, but I wager my body, my life, against your property that the dragons die."

Then began a great conflict along the banks and in the swift waters. Hiiaka struck the dragons with her magic skirt in which was concealed the divine power of lightning. They tried to escape, but Hiiaka struck again and again and killed them, changing the bodies into blocks of stone. Then she called the chief, saying, "I have made the way safe for your people and you; I give back your property and the land of the dragons."

Hiiaka and her friends turned north again and hastened to Waipio Valley to catch Mahiki—the demon of the whirlwind. He ran down to meet her and threw dust all over them, then fled inland to the mountains. Hiiaka chanted:

"I am above Waipio,
My eyes look sharply down.

I have gone along the path
By the sea of Makaukiu,
Full flowing like the surf.
I have seen Mahiki,
I have seen that he is evil,
Evil, very evil indeed."

Moo-Lau

THEN HIIAKA THOUGHT OF MOO-LAU, who was the great dragon-god of the district Kohala. He had a great multitude of lesser gods as his servants.

Hiiaka clearly and sweetly called for the dragon-gods to prepare a way for her and also to bring gifts for herself and her companions.

Moo-lau answered, "You have no path through my lands unless you have great strength or can pay the price."

Then began one of the great legendary battles of ancient Hawaiian folk-lore. Hiiaka, throwing aside her flower-wreaths and common clothes, took her lightning pa-u (skirt) and attacked Moo-lau. He fought her in his dragon form. He breathed fierce winds against her. He struck her with his swift-moving tail. He tried to catch her between his powerful jaws, He coiled and twisted and swiftly whirled about, trying to knock her down, but she beat him with her powerful hands in which dwelt some of the divine power of volcanoes. She struck his great body with her magic skirt in which dwelt the power of the lightning. Each pitted supernatural powers against the other. Each struck with magic force and each threw out magic strength to ward off deadly blows. They became tired, very tired, and, turning away from each other, sought rest. Again they fought and again rested.

Hiiaka chanted an incantation, or call for help:

"Moo-lau has a dart
Of the wood of the uhi-uhi;[1]
A god is Moo-lau, Moo-lau is a god!"

This was a spirit-call going out from Hiiaka. It broke through the clouds hanging on the sides of the mountains. It pierced the long, long

---

1. Smilax Sandwicensis.

way to the crater of Kilauea. It roused the followers of the fire-goddess. A host of destructive forces, swift as lightning, left the pit of fire to aid Hiiaka.

Meanwhile Moo-lau had sent his people to spy out the condition of Hiiaka. Then he called for all the reptile gods of his district to help him. He rallied all the gnomes and evil powers he could order to come to his aid and make a mighty attack.

When the battle seemed to be going against her, suddenly the Ho-ai-ku men and the Ho-ai-ka women, the destructive gnomes from the crater, broke in a storm upon Moo-lau and his demons. Oh, how the little people from the pit devoured and destroyed the dragon army! The slaughter of the reptile horde was quickly accomplished and Hiiaka soon saw the body of her enemy the dragon-god trampled underfoot.

When the god Mahiki saw that Moo-lau was slain and his army defeated he raised a great cloud of dust and fled far off around the western side of the island. The whirlwind was one of the earth-monsters which even the sister of the goddess of volcanoes could not destroy.

Many were the evil demi-gods who tried to hinder Hiiaka in her journey along the east coast of the island Hawaii. Sharks fought her from the seas. The gnomes and dragons of valley and forest tried to destroy her. Even birds of evil omen came into the fight against her, but she conquered and killed until the land was freed from its enemies and the people of the districts along the sea could journey in comparative safety.

Pau-o-palae, the goddess of ferns, met the chief of this land which had been freed from the power of the dragon. She saw him swimming in the sea and, forgetting her companions, leaped in to sport with him. They at once decided to be married. Then she turned aside to his new home, leaving Hiiaka and Wahine-omao to go on after Lohiau.

XVII

LOHIAU

The story of Hiiaka's journey over the seas which surround the Hawaiian Islands, and through dangers and perplexities, cannot be fully told in the limits of these short stories. There are several versions, so only the substance of all can be given.

On each island she slew dragons which had come from the ancient traditional home of the Polynesians, India. She destroyed many evil-minded gnomes and elves; fought the au-makuas and the demi-gods of land and sea; found the body of Lohiau put away in a cave and watched over by the dragon-women who had been defeated by, Pele when in her long sleep she chanted the songs of the Winds of Kauai. She slew the guardians of the cave, carried the body to a house where she used powerful chants for restoration. She captured the wandering ghost of Lohiau and compelled it again to take up its home in the body, and then with Lohiau and Wahine-omao made the long journey to her home in the volcano. From the island of Hawaii to the island Kauai, and along the return journey Hiiaka's path was marked with experiences beneficial to the people whom she passed. This must all be left untold except the story of Lohiau's restoration of life and the conflict with Pele.

As Hiiaka and her friend came near the island Kauai, Hiiaka told Wahine-omao that Lohiau was dead and that she saw the spirit standing by the opening of a cave out on the pali of Haena.

Then she chanted to Lohiau:

> *"The lehua is being covered by the sand,*
> *A little red flower remains on the plain,*
> *The body is hidden in the stones,*
> *The flower is lying in the path.*
> *Very useful is the water of Kaunu."*

Thus she told the ghost that site would give new life even as dew on a thirsty flower. They landed and met Lohiau's sisters and friends.

Hiiaka asked about the death of Lohiau, and one sister said, "His breath left him and the body became yellow." Hiiaka said: "There was no real reason for death, but the two women dragons took his spirit and held it captive. I will try to bring him back. Great is the magic power and strength of the two dragons and I am not a man, and may not win the victory. I will have something to eat, and then will go. You must establish a tabu for twenty days, and there must be quiet. No one can go to the mountains, nor into the sea. You must have a house made of ti[1] leaves for the dead body and make it very tight on all sides."

The next day they made the house. Hiiaka commanded that a door be made toward the east. Then Hiiaka said, "Let us open the door of the house." When this was done, Hiiaka said: "Tomorrow let the tabu be established on land and sea. Tomorrow we commence our work."

She made arrangements to go to the cave in the precipice at dawn. Rain came down in floods and a strong wind swept the face of the precipice. A fog clung fast to the hills. The water rushed in torrents to the sea. It was an evil journey to Lohiau.

At sunrise they went on through the storm. Hiiaka uttered this incantation:

> "Our halas greet the inland precipice,
> In the front of the calling hill.
> Let it call,
> You are calling to me.
> Here is the great hill outside.
> It is cold,
> Cold for us."

The dragons shouted for them to stay down, or they would destroy them on the rocks. But the small spirit voice of Lohiau called for Hiiaka to come and get him.

Hiiaka chanted to Lohiau, telling him they would save him. As they went up, stones in showers fell around and upon them. One large stone struck Hiiaka in the breast, and she fell off the pali. Then they began to get up and sticks of all kinds fell upon them again, forcing Hiiaka over the precipice.

The dragons leaped down on Hiiaka, trying to catch her in their mouths and strike her with their tails. Hiiaka struck them with her magic skirt, and their bodies were broken.

---

1. Ti or ki or lauki, Cordyline terminalis.

W.D. WESTERVELT

The spirits of the dragons went into other bodies and leaped upon Hiiaka roaring, and biting and tearing her body. She swung her skirt up against the dragons, and burned their bodies to ashes. The dragons again took new bodies for the last and most bitter battle.

Hiiaka told Wahine-omao to cover her body with leaves and sticks near the pali and in event of her death to return with the tidings to Hawaii.

One dragon caught Hiiaka and bent her over. The other leaped upon Hiiaka, catching her around the neck and arm. One tried to Pull off the pa-u and tear it to pieces.

Pau-o-palae saw the danger. From her home on the island Hawaii, she saw the dragons shaking Hiiaka. Then she sent her power and took many kinds of trees and struck the dragons. The roots twisted around the dragons, entangling their feet and tails, and scratching eyes and faces.

The dragons tried to shake off the branches and roots—the leaf bodies of the wilderness, and one let go the pa-u of Hiiaka, and the other let go the neck. Pau-o-palae called all the wind bodies of the forest and sent them to aid Hiiaka, the forces of the forest, and the wind spirits.

At last Hiiaka turned to say farewell to Wahine-omao because the next fight with the dragons in their new bodies might prove fatal.

The dragons were now stronger than before. They leaped upon her, one on each side. The strong winds blew and the storm poured upon her, while the dragons struck her to beat her down. But all kinds of ferns were leaping up rapidly around the place where the dragons renewed the fight. The ferns twisted and twined around the legs and bodies of the dragons.

Hiiaka shook her magic skirt and struck them again and again, and the bodies of these dragons were broken in pieces. Then the wind ceased, the storm passed away, and the sky became clear. But it was almost evening and darkness was falling fast.

The natives have for many years claimed that Hiiaka found the time too short to climb the precipice, catch the ghost of Lohiau and carry it and the body down to the house prepared for her work, therefore she uttered this incantation:

> O gods! Come to Kauai, your land.
> O pearl-eyed warrior (an idol) of Halawa!
> O Kona! guardian of our flesh!
> O the great gods of Hiiaka!

Come, ascend, descend,
Let the sun stop over the river of Hea.
Stand thou still, O sun!"

The sun waited and its light rested on the precipice and pierced the deep shadows of the cave in which the body lay while Hiiaka sought Lohiau.

Hiiaka heard the spirit voice saying, "Moving, moving, you will find me in a small coconut calabash fastened in tight." Hiiaka followed the spirit voice and soon saw a coconut closed up with feathers. Over the coconut a little rainbow was resting. She caught the coconut and went back to the body of Lohiau. It had become very dark in the cave, but she did not care, this was as nothing to her. She took the bundle of the body of Lohiau and said: "We have the body and the spirit, we are ready now to go down to our house."

Then she called the spirits of the many kinds of ferns of Pau-o-palae to take the body down. The fern servants of Pau-o-palae carried the bundle of the body down to the house.

Hiiaka said to her friend: "You ask how the spirit can be restored into the body. It is hard and mysterious and a work of the gods. We must gather all kinds of ferns and maile and lehua and flowers from the mountains. We must take wai-lua (flowing water) and wai-lani (rain) and put them into new calabashes to use in washing the body. Then pray. If my prayer is not broken (interrupted or a mistake made), he will be alive. If the prayer is broken four times, life will not return."

The servants of Pau-o-palae, the goddess of ferns, brought all manner of sweet-scented ferns, flowers, and leaves to make a bed for the body of Lohiau, and to place around the inside of the house as fragrant paths by which the gods could come to aid the restoration to life.

There were many prayers, sometimes to one class of gods and sometimes to another. The following prayer was offered to the au-makuas, or ghost-gods, residing in cloud-land and revealing themselves in different cloud forms:

"Dark is the prayer rising up to Kanaloa,
Rising up to the ancient home Kealohilani.
Look at the kupuas above sunset!
Who are the kupuas above?
The black dog of the heavens,

The yellow dog of Ku in the small cloud,
Ku is in the long cloud,
Ku is in the short cloud,
Ku is in the cloud of red spots in the sky.
Listen to the people of the mountains,
The friends of the forest, The voices of the heavens.
The water of life runs, life is coming,
Open with trembling, to let the spirit in,
A noise rumbling,
The sound of Ku.
The lover sent for is coming.
I, Hiiaka, am coming.
The lover of my sister Pele,
The sister of life,
Is coming to life again.
Live, Live."

After each one of the prayers and incantations the body was washed in the kind of water needed for each special ceremony, Thus days passed by; some legends say ten days, some say a full month. At last the body was ready for the incoming of the spirit.

The coconut shell in which the spirit had been kept was held against the body, the feet and limbs were slapped, and the body rubbed by Wahine-omao while Hiiaka continued her necessary incantations until the restoration to life was complete.

Many, many days had passed since the fiery and impetuous Pele had sent her youngest sister after the lover Lohiau. In her restlessness Pele had torn up the land in all directions around the pit of fire with violent earthquakes. She had poured her wrath in burning floods of lava over all the southern part of the island. She had broken her most solemn promise to Hiiaka.

Whenever she became impatient at the delay of the coming of Lohiau, she would fling her scorching smoke and foul gas over Hiiaka's beautiful forests—and sometimes would smite the land with an overflow of burning lava.

Sometimes she would look down over that part of Puna where Hopoe dwelt and hurl spurts of lava toward her home. At last she had yielded to her jealous rage and destroyed Hopoe and her home and then burned the loved spots of restful beauty belonging to Hiiaka.

Hiiaka had seen Pele's action as she had looked back from time to time on her journey to Kauai. Even while she was bringing Lohiau back to life, her love for her own home revealed to her the fires kindled by Pele, and she chanted many songs of complaint against her unfaithful sister.

Hiiaka loyally fulfilled her oath until she stood with Lohiau on one of the high banks overlooking Ka-lua-Pele, the pit of Pele in the volcano Kilauea. Down below in the awful majesty of fire were the sisters.

Wahine-omao went down to them as a messenger from Hiiaka. One of the legends says that Pele killed her; another says that she was repulsed and driven away; others say that Pele refused to listen to any report of the journey to Kauai and hurled Wahine-omao senseless into a hole near the fire-pit, and raved against Hiiaka for the long time required in bringing Lohiau.

Hiiaka at last broke out in fierce rebellion against Pele. On the hill where they stood were some of the lehua trees with their brilliant red blossoms. She plucked the flowers, made wreaths, and going close to Lohiau hung them around his neck.

All through the long journey to the crater Lohiau had been gaining a full appreciation of the bravery, the unselfishness, and the wholly lovable character of Hiiaka. He had proposed frequently that they be husband and wife, Now as they stood on the brink of the crater with all the proof of Pele's oath-breaking around them Hiiaka gave way entirely. She chanted while she fastened the flowers tightly around him and while her arms were playing around his neck:

> *"Hiiaka is the wife.*
> *Caught in the embrace with the flowers.*
> *The slender thread is fast.*
> *Around him the leis from the land of the lehuas are fastened.*
> *I am the wife—The clouds are blown down*
> *Hiding the sea at Hilo."*

Lohiau had no longer any remnant of affection for Pele. Hiiaka had fulfilled her vow and Pele had broken all her promises. Lohiau and Hiiaka were now husband and wife. Pele had lost forever her husband of the long sleep.

Pele was uncontrollable in her jealous rage. One of the legends says that even while Lohiau and Hiiaka were embracing each other Pele ran up the hill and threw her arms around his feet and black lava congealed

W.D. WESTERVELT

over them, Then she caught his knees and then his body. Lava followed every clasp of the arms of Pele, until at last his whole body was engulfed in a lava flow. His spirit leaped from the body into some clumps of trees and ferns not far away.

Another legend says that Pele sent her brother Lono-makua, with his helpers, to kindle eruptions around Lohiau and Hiiaka. This could not harm Hiiaka, for she was at home in the worst violence of volcanic flames, but it meant death to Lohiau.

Lono-makua kindled fires all around Lohiau, but for a long time refrained from attacking him.

Hiiaka could not see the pit as clearly as Lohiau, so she asked if Pele's fires were coming. He chanted:

"Hot is this mountain of the priest.

Rain is weeping on the awa.
I look over the rim of the crater.
Roughly tossing is the lava below.
Coming up to the forest—
Attacking the trees—
Clouds of smoke from the crater."

The lava came up, surrounding them. Tossing fountains of lava bespattered them. Wherever any spot of his body was touched Lohiau became stone. He uttered incantations and used all his Powers as a sorcerer-chief. The lava found it difficult to overwhelm him. Pele sent increased floods of burning rock upon him. Lohiau's body was all turned to stone. His spirit fled from the pit to the cool places of a forest on a higher part of the surrounding mountains.

Hiiaka was crazed by the death of Lohiau. She had fought against the eruption; now she caught the lava, tore it to pieces, and broke down the walls toward the innermost depths of their lava home. She began to open the pit for the coming of the sea.

Pele and her sisters were frightened. Pele called Wahine-omao from her prison and listened to the story of Hiiaka's faithfulness. Chagrined and full of self-blame, she told Wahine-omao how to restore happiness to her friend.

Wahine-omao went to Hiiaka and softly chanted by the side of the crazy one who was breaking up the pit. She told the story of the journey after Lohiau and the possibility of seeking the wandering ghost.

Hiiaka turned from the pit and sought Lohiau. Many were the adventures in ghost-land. At last the ghost was found. Lohiau's body was freed from the crust of lava and healed and the ghost put back in its former home. A second time Hiiaka had given life to Lohiau.

Hiiaka and Lohiau went to Kauai, where, as chief and chiefess, they lived happily until real death came to Lohiau.

THEN HIIAKA RETURNED TO HER place in the Pele family. It was said that Wahine-omao became the wife of Lono-makua, the one kindling volcanic fire.

XVIII

The Annihilation of Keoua's Army

Almost exactly thirty-four years before Kapiolani defied the worship of the fire-goddess Pele, Keoua, a high chief, lost a large part of his army near the volcano Kilauea. This was in November, 1790.

Ka-lani-opuu had been king over the island Hawaii. When he died in 1782, he left the kingdom to his son Kiwalao, giving the second place to his nephew Kamehameha.

War soon arose between the cousins. Kamehameha defeated and killed the young king. Kiwalao's half-brother Keoua escaped to his district Ka-u, on the southwestern side of the island. His uncle Keawe-mau-hili escaped to his district Hilo on the southeastern side.

For some years the three factions practically let each other alone, although there was desultory fighting. Then the high chief of Hilo accepted Kamehameha as his king and sent his sons to aid Kamehameha in conquering the island Maui.

Keoua was angry with his uncle Keawe-mau-hili. He attacked Hilo, killed his uncle and ravaged Kamehameha's lands along the northeastern side of the island.

Kamehameha quickly returned from Maui and made an immediate attack on his enemy, who had taken possession of a fertile highland plain called Waimea. From this method of forcing unexpected battle came the Hawaiian saying, "The spear seeks Waimea like the wind."

Keoua was defeated and driven through forests along the eastern side of Mauna Kea (The white mountain) to Hilo. Then Kamehameha sent warriors around the western side of the island to attack Keoua's home district. Meanwhile, after a sea fight in which he defeated the chiefs of the islands Maui and Oahu, he set his people to building a great temple chiefly for his war-god Ka-ili. This was the last noted temple built on all the islands.

Keoua heard of the attack on his home, therefore he gave the fish-ponds and fertile lands of Hilo to some of his chiefs and hastened to cross the island with his army by way of a path near the volcano Kilauea. He divided his warriors into three parties, taking charge of the first in person. They passed the crater at a time of great volcanic activity. A native writer, probably Kamakau, in the native newspaper *Kuokoa*, 1867, describes the destruction of the central part of this army by an awful explosion from Kilauea.

He said: "Thus was it done. Sand, ashes, and stones grew up from the pit into a very high column of fire, standing straight up. The mountains of Mauna Kea and Mauna Loa were below it. The people even from Ka-wai-hae (a seaport on the opposite side of the mountains) saw this wonderful column with fire glowing and blazing to its very top. When this column became great it blew all to pieces into sand and ashes and great stones, which for some days continued to fall around the sides of Kilauea. Men, women, and children were killed. Mona, one of the army, who saw all this but who escaped, said that one of the chiefesses was ill and some hundreds of the army had delayed their journey to guard her and so escaped this death."

Dibble, the first among the missionaries to prepare a history of the islands, gave the following description of the event:

"Keoua's path led by the great volcano of Kilauea. There they encamped. In the night a terrific eruption took place, throwing out flame, cinders, and even heavy stones to a great distance and accompanied from above with intense lightning and heavy thunder. In the morning Keoua and his companions were afraid to proceed and spent the day in trying to appease the goddess of the volcano, whom they supposed they had offended the day before by rolling stones into the crater. But on the second night and on the third night also there were similar eruptions. On the third day they ventured to proceed on their way, but had not advanced far before a more terrible and destructive eruption than any before took place; an account of which, taken from the lips of those who were part of the company and present in the scene, may not be an unwelcome digression.

'The army of Keoua set out on their way in three different companies. The company in advance had not proceeded far before the ground began to shake and rock beneath their feet and it became quite impossible to stand. Soon a dense cloud of darkness was seen to rise out of the crater, and almost at the same instant the electrical effect upon the air was so great that the thunder began to roar in the heavens and the lightning to flash. It continued to ascend and spread abroad until the whole region was enveloped and the light of day was entirely excluded. The darkness was the more terrific, being made visible by an awful glare from streams of red and blue light variously combined that issued from the pit below, and being lit up at intervals by the intense flashes of lightning from above. Soon followed an immense volume of sand and cinders which were thrown in high heaven and came down in a destructive shower for many miles around. Some few persons of the forward company were burned to death by the sand and cinders and others were seriously injured. All experienced a suffocating sensation upon the lungs and hastened on with all possible speed.

'The rear body, which was nearest the volcano at the time of the eruption, seemed to suffer the least injury, and after the earthquake and shower of sand had passed over, hastened forward to escape the dangers which threatened them, and rejoicing in mutual congratulations that they had been preserved in the midst of such imminent peril.

'But what was their surprise and consternation when, on coming up with their comrades of the centre party, they discovered them all to have become corpses. Some were lying down, and others sitting upright clasping with dying grasp their wives and children and joining noses (their form of expressing affection) as in the act of taking a final leave. So much like life they looked that they at first supposed them merely at rest, and it was not until they had come up to them and handled them that they could detect their mistake. Of the whole party, including women and children, not one of them survived to relate the catastrophe that had befallen their comrades. The only living being they found was a solitary hog, in company with one of the families which had been so suddenly bereft of life. In those perilous circumstances, the surviving party did not even stay to bewail their fate, but, leaving their deceased companions as they found them, hurried on and overtook the company in advance at the place of their encampment.'

"Keoua and his followers, of whom the narrator of this scene were a part, retreated in the direction they had come. On their return, they found their deceased friends as they had left them, entire and exhibiting no other marks of decay than a sunken hollowness in their eyes; the rest of their bodies was in a state of entire preservation. They were never buried, and their bones lay bleaching in the sun and rain for many years."

A blast of sulphurous gas, a shower of heated embers, or a volume of heated steam would sufficiently account for this sudden death. Some of the narrators who saw the corpses affirm that, though in no place deeply burnt, yet they were thoroughly scorched."

Keoua's prophets ascribed this blow from the gods to their high chief's dislike of Hilo and gift to sub-chiefs of the fish-ponds, which were considered the favorite food-producers for offerings to Hiiaka, the youngest member of the Pele family.

Kamehameha's prophets said that this eruption was the favor of the gods on his temple building.

The people said it was proof that Pele had taken Kamehameha under her especial protection and would always watch over his interests and make him the chief ruler.

XIX

Destruction of Kamehameha's Fish-Ponds

Mount Hualalai is on the western side of the island Hawaii. It has been announced as an extinct volcano because few signs of volcanic life appear at present; but in the year 1801 there was a very violent eruption from the foot of the mountain, and the expectation of future action is so strong that scientists classify Hualalai as "active."

Ellis, writing in 1824, says: "This eruption of 1801 poured over several villages, destroyed a number of plantations and extensive fish-ponds, filled up a deep bay twenty miles in length, and formed the present coast. An Englishman who saw the eruption has frequently told us that he was astonished at the irresistible impetuosity of the torrent. Stone walls, trees, and houses all gave way before it. Even large masses or rocks of ancient lava, when surrounded by the fiery stream, soon split into small fragments and falling into the burning mass appeared to melt again while borne by it down the mountain side.

Numerous offerings were presented and many hogs were thrown into the stream to appease the anger of the gods, by whom they supposed it was directed, and to stay its devastating course. All seemed unavailing until one day King Kamehameha went to the flowing lava, attended by a large retinue of chiefs and priests, and as the most valuable offering he could make, cut off part of his own hair which was always considered sacred and threw it into the torrent. In a day or two the lava ceased to flow. The gods, it was thought, were satisfied. The people attributed this escape to the influence of Kamehameha with the deities of the volcanoes."

There are several very interesting "blowholes" in this lava. When the lava struck the waves, the surface and sides were hardened, but the red molten mass inside rolled on into the sea. Thus many sea-caves were formed, in to which waves beat violently with every incoming tide. If the shore end of a cave broke open, a fine out let was made for the torrents which were hurled up through the opening in splendid fountains of spray.

The account in the *Kuokoa*, a newspaper published in the native language, in 1867, adds to the story of the foreigner the element of superstition, and is practically as follows:

Pele began to eat Hue-hue, a noted breadfruit[1] forest owned by Kamehameha. She was jealous of him and angry because he was stingy in his offerings of breadfruit from the tabu grove of Hue-hue. This was the place where the eruption broke out.

After she had destroyed the breadfruit grove, she went in her river of fire down to the seashore to take Kamehameha's fish-ponds. She greatly desired the awa fish with the mullet in the fish-pond at Kiholo, and she wanted the aku or bonita in the fish-pond at Ka-ele-hulu-hulu. She became a roaring flood, widely spread out, hungry for the fish.

Kamehameha was very much ashamed for the evil which had come upon the land and the destruction of his fish-ponds. Villages had been overwhelmed. Several coconut[2] groves had been destroyed, and lava land was built out into the sea.

There were no priests who could stop this a-a eruption by their priestly skill. Their powers were dulled in the presence of Pele. They offered pigs and fruits of all kinds, throwing them into the fire. They uttered all their known incantations and prayers. They called to the au-makuas (ancestor ghost-gods), but without avail.

Kamehameha sent for Ka-maka-o-ke-akua (The-eye-of-the-god), one of the prophets of Pele, and said: "You are a prophet of Pele. I have sent for you because I am much distressed by the destruction of the land and the ponds by the sea. How can I quiet the anger of Pele?"

The prophet bowed his head for a time, then, looking up, said, "The anger of the god will cease when you offer sacrifice to her."

The king said, "Perhaps you will take the sacrifice."

The prophet said: "From the old time even until now there has been no prophet or priest of the mo-o or dragon clan who has done this thing. It would not please the goddess. The high chief of the troubled land, with a prophet or priest, is the only one who can make peace. He must take his own offering to the fire as to an altar in a temple. Then the anger of the goddess will be satisfied and the trouble ended."

Kamehameha said: "I am afraid of Pele. Perhaps I shall be killed."

The prophet replied, "You shall not die."

The king prepared offerings and sacrifices for Pele and, as a royal priest, went to the place where the lava was still pouring in floods out of its new-born crater.

---

1. Native ulu = Artocarpus incisa.
2. Cocos nucifera.

Kaahumanu, the queen, and many other high chiefs and chiefesses thought they would go and die with him if Pele should persist in punishing him. One of the high chiefesses, Ululani, had lost a child some time before. This child after death was given to Pele with sacrifices and ceremonies which would make it one of the ghost-gods connected with the Pele family.

A prophet told Kaahumanu: "The Pele who is in the front of this outburst of fire is not strange to us. It is the child of Ululani."

Kaahumanu took Ululani with her to the side of the lava flow.

There they saw the lava like a river of fire flowing toward the west, going straight down to the sea with leaping flames and uplifting fountains of smoke. There was a very strong flashing light breaking out at the front of the descending lava.

Ululani asked, "Who is that very strange fire in front of Pele?" The fire was active as if it had life in itself.

The prophet replied: "That is the child among the au-makuas. That is your first-born."

Then came great winds and a mighty storm. Houses were overturned and trees blown down.

Kamehameha and the prophet went up to the side of the lava and placed offerings and sacrifices in the flowing fire. They prayed to Pele, but the fire burned on. Kamehameha then cut some of the hair from his head and threw it in the fire as his last offering, thus giving himself to the god of fire. Then they came away and soon the fire went out.

It should be remembered that in recent years, when a lava flow came down on the city of Hilo, threatening its destruction, Princess Ruth, one of the last of the Kamehameha family, went from Honolulu to Hilo and up to the river of lava with the feeling that a Kamehameha who was under the especial protection of Pele could intercede for the welfare of the people. It is certain that she came at a very opportune time, for the eruption ceased in a day or so.

XX

Kapiolani and Pele

The story of the high chiefess Kapiolani and her conflict with Pele, the goddess of Kilauea, in December, 1824, is historic. It belongs, however, to the volcanoes of the Hawaiian Islands, and is more important than any myth.

Kapiolani was the daughter of Keawe-mau-hili, who was the high chief of the district of Hilo. He was the uncle of Kiwalao, the young king of the island Hawaii, who was killed by Kamehameha's warriors when Kamehameha became king of that island.

Kapiolani as a little child was in the camp with her father at the time of the battle. She was in danger of death, but some men carried her over the mountains through a multitude of difficulties back to Hilo. She became a tall, portly woman, with keen black eyes and an engaging countenance, a queen in appearance when with other chiefs or chiefesses. She was not a queen, nor was she even a princess, although by blood relationship she belonged to the royal family. She was the wife of Na-ihe, who was the high chief of the district of Kona on the western side of the island Hawaii.

Na-ihe (The spears) was said to be the national orator or best speaker on government affairs among the chiefs. Kapiolani (The-bending-arch-of-heaven) was very intelligent, quick-witted, and fearless. They were both so influential that they were chosen by the great Kamehameha, as members of his council of chiefs and were retained by his son Liholiho, or Kamehameha II.

When the missionaries of the American Board from Boston arrived, April 4, 1820, at Kailua Bay on the western coast of Hawaii, they landed in territory nominally controlled by Na-ihe and Kapiolani, although at that particular time the young king, Liholiho, and his court were in Kona, and were the real rulers.

However, when the missionaries had reduced the language to writing and had begun to print leaflets for spelling and reading, in 1822, Na-ihe and Kapiolani were among the first chiefs to welcome instruction and accept Christianity as far as they could understand it.

In 1823 a delegation of missionaries went around the island Hawaii.

They visited the volcano Kilauea and wrote the first really good description of the crater and its activity. The natives were astonished to see the perfect safety of the missionaries, although the worship and tabus of Pele were absolutely ignored. Ohelo[1] berries and strawberries growing on the brink of the crater were freely eaten and the lake of fire explored without even a thought of fear of the goddess.

In the course of their journey the missionaries met a priestess of Pele. The priestess, assuming a haughty air, said: "I am Pele, I shall never die. Those who follow me, if part of their bones are taken to Kilauea, will live in the bright fire there." A missionary said, "Are you Pele?" She said, "Yes, I am Pele," then proceeded to state her powers. A chief of low rank who had been a royal messenger under Kamehameha, and who was making the journey with the missionaries, interrupted the woman, saying: "Then it is true, you are Pele, and have destroyed the land, killed the people, and have spoiled the fishing-grounds. If I were the king I would throw you into the sea." The priestess was quick-witted and said that truly she had done some harm, but the rum of the foreigners was far more destructive.

All this prepared the way for Kapiolani to attempt to break down the worship of the fire-goddess. It must be remembered that Kapiolani had been under the influence of thoughtful civilization only about three years when she decided that she would attack the idolatry which, of all idol worship, was the most firmly entrenched in the hearts of her people because it was founded on the mysterious forces of nature. She accepted implicitly the word of the missionaries, that their God was the one god of nature. Therefore she had rejected the fire-goddess with all the other deities formerly worshipped in Hawaii. She was, however, practically alone in her determination to strike a blow against the worship of Pele.

Priests of Pele were numerous on the island Hawaii. Women were among those of highest rank in that priesthood. Many of the personal followers of Kapiolani were worshippers. Even Na-ihe, her husband, had not been able to free himself from superstitious fears. When Kapiolani said that she was going to prove the falsity of the worship of Pele, there was a storm of heartfelt opposition. The priests and worshippers of Pele honestly believed that divine punishment would fall on her. Those who were Christians were afraid that some awful explosion might overwhelm

1. Vaccinium penduliformis—var. reticulatum.

the company, as a large body of warriors had been destroyed thirty-four years before.

Na-ihe, still strongly under the influence of superstition, urged her not to go. All this opposition arose from her warm friends. When her determination was seen to be immovable, some of the priests of Pele became bitterly angry and in their rage prophesied most awful results.

When Kapiolani left her home in Kona her people, with great wailing, again attempted to persuade her to stay with them. The grief, stimulated by fear of things supernatural, was uncontrollable. The people followed their chiefess some distance with prayers and tears.

For more than a hundred miles she journeyed, usually walking, sometimes having a smooth path, but again having to cross miles of the roughest, most rugged and sharp-edged lava on the island Hawaii. At last the party came to the vicinity of the volcano. This was not by the present road, but along the smoother, better way, used for centuries on the south side of the crater toward the ocean.

Toward the close of the day they crossed steaming cracks and chasms and drew nearer to the foul-smelling, gaseous clouds of smoke which blew toward them from the great crater. Here a priestess of Pele of the highest rank came to meet the party and turn them away from the dominions of the fire-goddess unless they would offer appropriate sacrifices. She knew Kapiolani's purpose, and determined to frustrate it.

Formerly there had been a temple near the brink of the crater on the southeast side. This, according to Ellis, bore the name Oala-laua. He says, "It was a temple of Pele, of which Ka-maka-a-ke-akua (The-eye-of-God), a distinguished soothsayer who died in the reign of Kamehameha, was many years priest." The temple was apparently deserted at the time of the overthrow of the tabu in 1819, and the priests had gone to the lower and better cultivated lands of Puna, where they had their headquarters. However, they still worshipped Pele and sacrificed to her.

This priestess who faced Kapiolani was very haughty and bold. She forbade her to approach any nearer to the volcano on pain of death at the hands of the furious goddess Pele.

"Who are you?" asked Kapiolani.

"I am one in whom the God dwells."

"If God dwells in you, then you are wise and can teach me. Come and sit down."

The priestess had seen printed pages or heard about them, so she drew out a piece of kapa, or paper made from the bark of trees,[2] and saying that this was a letter from Pele began to read or rather mumble an awful curse.

The people with Kapiolani were hushed into a terrified silence, but she listened quietly until the priestess, carried beyond her depth, read a confused mass of jumbled words, and unintelligible noises, which she called "The dialect of the ancient Pele."

Then Kapiolani took her spelling-book, and a little book of a few printed hymns, and said: "You have pretended to deliver a message from your god, but we have not understood it. Now I will read you a message which you can understand, for I, too, have a letter." Then she read clearly the Biblical sentences printed in the spelling-book and some of the hymns. The priestess was silenced.

Meanwhile, the missionaries at Hilo, a hundred and fifty miles from Kona, heard that Kapiolani had started on this strenuous undertaking. They felt that some one of the Christian teachers should be with her. Mr. Ruggles had been without shoes for several months and could not go. Mr. Goodrich, the other missionary stationed at Hilo, was almost as badly off, but was more accustomed to travelling barefoot. So he went up through the tangled masses of sharp-edged lava, grass, strong-leaved ferns, and thick woods to meet the chiefess as she came to the crater.

Kapiolani passed the priestess, went on to the crater, met Mr. Goodrich, and was much affected by the effort he had made to aid her in her attempt to break down the worship of Pele. It was now evening, and a hut was built to shelter her until the next day came, when she could have the opportunity of descending into the crater.

Mr. Richards, a missionary, later wrote as follows: "Along the way to the volcano she was accosted by multitudes and entreated not to proceed. She answered, 'If I am destroyed, then you may all believe in Pele, but if I am not, you must all turn to the true writings.'"

The great crater at that time had a black ledge or shelf, below which the active lakes and fountains of fire, in many places, broke through and kept turbulent a continually changing mass over five miles in circumference. Here in the large cones built up by leaping lava, the natives said, were the homes of the family of Pele. Here the deities amused themselves in

---

2. Plants used for kapa were wauke, olona, mamaki, poulu, akala, hau, maaloa, and the mulberry.

games. The roaring of the furnaces and crackling of flames was the music of drums beaten for the accompaniment of the household dances. The red flaming surge was the surf wherein they played.

As the morning light brought a wonderful view of the Lua Pele (The-pit-of-Pele) with its great masses of steam and smoke rising from the immense field of volcanic activity below, and as the rush of mighty waves of lava broke again and again against the black ledge with a roar exceeding that of a storm-driven surf beating upon rocky shores, and as fierce explosions of gases bursting from the underworld in a continual cannonade, deafened the ears of the company, Kapiolani prepared to go down to defy Pele.

This must have been one of the few grand scenes of history. There was the strong, brave convert to Christianity standing above the open lake of fire, the red glowing lava rolling in waves below, with rough blocks of hardened lava on every side, the locks (Pele's hair) of the fire-goddess, torn out and whirling around in the air, the timid fearful faces of the people and their attitude of terror and anxiety showing the half-hope that the tabu might be broken and the half-dread lest the evil spirit might breathe fire upon them and destroy them at once.

Mr. Richards says: "A man whose duty it was to feed Pele, by throwing berries and the like into the volcano, entreated her to go no farther. 'And what,' said she, 'will be the harm?' The man replied, 'You will die by Pele.' Kapiolani answered, 'I shall not die by your god. That fire was kindled by my God.' The man was silent and she went onward, descending several hundred feet, and there joined in a prayer to Jehovah. She also ate the berries consecrated to Pele, and threw stones into the volcano."

Bingham in his "Sandwich Islands" says: "Then with the terrific bellowing and whizzing of the volcanic gases they mingled their voices in a solemn hymn of praise to the true God, and at the instance of the chiefess, Alapai, one of Kapiolani's attendants, led them in prayer."

The party returned to the brink of the crater, and journeyed down to Hilo.

Alexander in the "History of the Hawaiian People" says, "This has justly been called one of the greatest acts of moral courage ever performed."

Richards states that the leader of Kapiolani's party said to him: "All the people of the district saw that she was not injured and have pronounced Pele to be powerless."

The influence of Kapiolani against this most influential form of idolatrous worship was felt throughout the whole nation.

In 1836, twelve years later, Rev. Titus Coan wrote about the coming of many natives into a Christian life. He says: "In 1836, twelve years after the visit of Kapiolani, among these converts was the High Priest of the volcano, He was more than six feet tall, and was of lofty bearing. He had been an idolater, a drunkard, an adulterer, a robber, and a murderer. His sister was more haughty and stubborn. She, too, was tall and majestic in her bearing. At length she yielded and with her brother became a docile member of the church."

But it was Lord Tennyson who set down for posterity the heroic deed of the great queen in the following beautiful poem:

KAPIOLANI

I

*When from the terrors of Nature a people have fashion'd
and worship a Spirit of Evil
Blest be the Voice of the Teacher who calls to them,
"Set yourselves free!"*

II

*Noble the Saxon who hurled at his Idol a valorous weapon
in olden England!
Great, and greater, and greatest of women, island heroine Kapiolani
Clomb the mountain, and flung the berries and dared
the Goddess, and freed the people
Of Hawa-i-ee!*

III

*A people believing that Peelè the Goddess would wallow
in fiery riot and revel
On Kilauea,
Dance in a fountain of flame with her devils or shake with her
thunders and shatter her island,
Rolling her anger
Thro' blasted valley and flowing forest in blood-red
cataracts down to the sea!*

IV

Long as the lava-light
Glares from the lava-take,
Dazing the starlight;
Long as the silvery vapor in daylight,
Over the mountain
Floats, will the glory of Kapiolani be mingled
with either on Hawa-i-ee.

V

What said her Priesthood?
"Woe to this island if ever a woman should handle or gather
the berries of Peelè
Accursed were she!
And woe to this island if ever a woman should climb to
the dwelling of Peelè the Goddess!
Accursed were she!"

VI

One from the Sunrise
Dawned on His people and slowly before him
Vanished shadow-like
Gods and Goddesses,
None but the terrible Peelè remaining as Kapiolani
Ascended her mountain,
Baffled her priesthood,
Broke the Taboo,
Dipt to the crater,
Called on the Power adored by the Christian and crying,
"I dare her, let Peelè avenge herself!"
Into the flame-billows dashed the berries, and drove
the demon from Hawa-i-ee.

PART II

GEOLOGICAL FACTS

(*Note*: The following articles pertaining to the geological formation of the Hawaiian Islands were written by the author at different times for the various local periodicals in Honolulu and will be found interesting by those who wish to increase their knowledge of volcanology.)

I

THE CRACK IN THE FLOOR OF THE PACIFIC

G eological or earthquake map of the Pacific shows that the ocean is bordered by ranges of volcanic mountains on the American side, and by a long chain of volcanic islands, such as the Aleutian, Japanese, and Formosa islands along the coast of Asia. It is also clear that between America and Asia connected islands built up by volcanic action follow what appear to be cracks in the floor of the Pacific.

It is interesting to note the fact that all along the western coast of North and South America there is only a comparatively narrow strip of land between the mountain ranges and the sea, and that from the edge of this narrow seacoast there is a rapid descent in the ocean bed until it becomes one of the most profound oceanic depressions on the globe. The depth of the floor of the ocean is greater than the enormous elevation of the mountain ranges along its edge. "The Challenger" surveyors give the average depth of the Pacific Ocean as about 2,400 fathoms, while between the Caroline and Ladrone groups of islands lies a valley whose ooze-carpeted floor can be reached only by a sounding line about 25,000 feet long, and near Japan about 30,000 feet of line is needed to reach the bottom of one of the deepest pits on the globe.

The German survey ship "Planet" has made the deepest sounding thus far taken. About forty sea miles off the north coast of Mindanao, the largest and most southerly of the important islands of the Philippines, the "Planet" found a depth of 32,078 feet. In other words, the Pacific Ocean where the sounding was taken has a depth of 6.07 miles, exceeding by 482 feet the greatest depth hitherto known.

In 1901 the United States survey ship "Nero," while studying out a route for a cable line to the Philippines, made a sounding some distance to the southeast of the island of Guam of 31,596 feet, which beat the world's record for sea depth up to that time. This is a depth of 5.98 miles, and is known as the" Nero" deep. The surpassing sea depth now discovered may appropriately be named the "Planet" deep.

Out of these awful ocean depths have come the chains and groups of islands which form Polynesia. It seems absolutely necessary to recognize the cracks in the floor of the ocean through which the vast floods of lava were forced for the upbuilding of these islands. Even the coral polyps had to have the edge of a crater to work on while building the innumerable coral reefs of the Pacific.

No one knows what mighty conflicts were fought between the two eternal enemies, fire and water; nor does anyone know how long they fought while these islands were being built into mountains, but there must have been ages when the skies were filled with rolling masses of clouds of steam sent up through boiling, turbulent waters with awful explosions of escaping gases before the dry land appeared on the face of the deep. It has been the modern story of creation. There were boiling seas and skies always covered with vast masses of steam clouds, then ages of mountain building at the hands of chaotic fire-rock, and the subsequent ages of the disintegration of lava, forming soil for the coming of plant and animal life.

The building of these islands has been a most stupendous task, and the chains of islands resulting from the tremendous volcanic energy still exhibit immense activity. The volcanic outbreaks and earthquakes of the Japanese islands from Nippon to Formosa are so frequent as to afford an excellent field for study. The New Zealand islands have a volcanic region around Roturua which is visited by numbers of tourists every year.

Islands appear and disappear in the Western Pacific. None of the islands have so good a tradition of these turbulent times as the Hawaiian group, and they have only a statement made by William Ellis in his book, "A Tour through Hawaii," published in 1826. He says that while on this tour around the island Hawaii, he stopped with John Young, who is now stated to have been an American sailor and a close friend of the great king Kamehameha I "Mr. Young said that among many traditionary accounts of the origin of the island, one was that in former times, when there was nothing but sea, an immense bird settled on the water and laid an egg which soon bursting produced the island Hawaii."

It must be remembered that the Hawaiians also have the pulling up of the islands with a fishhook by the demi-god Maui, who fished up many islands in Polynesia.

It has been nearly a hundred years since Ellis made the brief reference to the production of an island by the explosion of the egg, and now it is impossible to secure any enlargement of the legend. The story stands as an ancient memory of volcanic activity so mighty and so extensive as to produce islands in the time of human experience.

II

Hawaiian Volcanoes

E ach island has its extinct craters from which extend the limited ranges of mountains and plains which make the island surface. These large craters are from a few hundred to over thirteen thousand feet in altitude. They seem to have had mighty explosions after they had been built into mountains, and one side of the crater has usually been blown out or has slid down into the ocean, leaving very high, steep side walls around irregularly shaped valleys opening toward the sea.

In these craters and between them and the sea are many small craters which mark the most recent eruptions on the various islands. There are no legends of the origin of any of these large craters, whether extinct or active. There are very interesting stories connected with many of them, and there are legends of the origin of some of the small extinct craters which lie at the bases of the mountain ranges. These usually are ascribed to the fire-goddess Pele, who came to the Hawaiian group ages after the islands were built, and who only succeeded in starting eruptions of no great importance until she found her present home in the volcano Kilauea. These small extinct craters marked the progress of Pele's journey through the islands.

The large mountains of all the islands, except Hawaii, have no hot springs and no outlets for steam or hot air which would indicate any remnant of living fire still abiding in them. Nor are there any very noticeable earthquake shocks in these other islands, even at the time when the island Hawaii is pouring floods of lava down its mountain sides and is shaking its inhabitants with great force.

Open volcanic activity is confined to the mountains of Hawaii. The mountains of Maui, especially Hale-a-ka-la, are called active because of historic eruptions and signs of hidden fire.

The extinct craters are very interesting. They have their broken-down side wall, through which the last great effort of volcanic life was poured out. They also have crater cones and sometimes lava flows of small extent on the floor left by the great eruption. These were the picturesque last throbs of life as a volcano died. Occasional spasmodic efforts were made in both earthquake and lava flow until the fire cooled in the submarine chambers.

From the summits of all these mountains, peculiarly fine cloud views can be enjoyed. There is not only the gathering of cloud masses rolling beneath the lover of the sublime,—this can be seen on all the large mountains of the world,—but here in the Hawaiian Islands the march of cloud armies sweeping over an ocean and spreading in ceaseless motion for miles over the lowlands receives an added element of majesty and awe when tossing, whirling cloud mountains roll into the extinct craters and slowly fill the bowl of the gods from rim to rim as the morning sun delicately touches the crater edges above the clouds with all the colors of the dawn.

Here and there in the decaying volcanic ash and disintegrating lava can sometimes be found beautiful, small, star-rayed zeolite, or the pale green olivine, or coarse black augite crystals. These are of no value, save as they show some of the forms taken by cooling lava, and are of interest chiefly to the scientist.

On the island Hawaii are three great mountains from 8,200 to 13,600 feet above the ocean, which smashes its mighty tides and surf waves against the coast below. One of these, Mauna Kea (White Mountain), is an extinct volcano with a lake of water in its crater. Hualalai is dormant, although from it there was a great eruption a little over a hundred years ago, and even now possibilities of activity are talked about by those who cultivate sugar-cane and coffee on its lower slopes. Mauna Loa (Great or long mountain) has a most interesting active crater on its summit, Mokuaweoweo (Blood-red island), from which enormous rivers of lava are hurled down to the waiting ocean many miles below.

What is said to be the most active crater in the world, Kilauea, lies on an eastern spur of Mauna Loa at an elevation of 4,000 feet above the sea. This crater is a great caldron or pit crater, and has been known among the Hawaiians for centuries as Ka-Lua Pele (The Pit of Pele). Below Kilauea are a number of craters of similar character, great sunken holes or pits in a country of almost even surface.

Kilauea is a surprise to the tourist. Ki-lau-ea means "the rising up or living leaf of the ti-plant." Ea means "to rise up" and also "to live." Ki-lau means "ti-leaf." A gradual ascent by rail and motor-car for about thirty miles brings the visitor to a flat region miles in extent and sparsely covered with giant ferns[1] and shrubs and gray-leaved trees with fringed red balls of flowers. Here and there small clouds of steam come from crevices around a hotel where the traveller finds his resting-place.

---

1. Tree fern—Cibotium Menziesii.

In front of this hotel, and not seen until the motor-car stops, is the crater whose edges are almost level with the surrounding plain. It is a precipice-walled bowl, three miles across, with a multitude of steam jets breaking through its vast floor and a great cloud of smoke rising from a pit in a black border-land of frozen lava. Kilauea looks like a congealed lake whose glossy black hard waves had hardened while rolling and struggling with each other under some fierce tempest. It is, however, a cone ascending gradually to the fire-pit from these precipitous edges of the bowl.

Under the smoke cloud of the pit lies the always active lake of fire, Ka-Lua Pele (The Pit of Pele), the traditional home of the goddess Pele, now called Halemaumau (House fixed or continuing).

From this volcano Kilauea, and the crater Mokuaweoweo, which lies like an island in the top of Mauna Loa, nearly 10,000 feet higher, come enormous and sometimes destructive lava flows. They are called rivers of lava, but a lava river, unlike a stream of water, flows underneath a continually cooling and hardening crumpled surface, pushing its way from under and at last leaving long tunnels. Sometimes new lava melts through the walls of these caves and pours along the path left ages before, frequently finding an outlet even under the waves of the sea. The natives say, "Pele has gone to the sea by the ala huna (the hidden path)." There are two kinds of lava which these rivers carry down. One in cooling becomes very smooth and hard. Its surface shines like black satin. Professor C. H. Hitchcock, the eminent geologist, says: "The name pa-hoe-hoe signifies having the aspect of satin or having a shining smooth surface. It is quite hummocky and shows a wrinkled ropy structure." The glossy part is real volcanic glass shining on the surface because the silica which is used in making glass rises to the top of the cooling lava. It is lighter than the other ingredients. This pa-hoe-hoe lava is abundant in the lava fields around Mexico City.

The name a-a, which signifies "torn up by roots," is the name given to another kind of lava. An a-a flow is lava changed into bristling, ragged rocks, with innumerable fine sharp edges cutting like fragments of broken glass. It appears very much like slag from iron furnaces, only infinitely worse to handle.

These two Hawaiian names are now the accepted scientific names for these classes of lava the world over.

In 1911 the first successful attempt to secure the temperature of the boiling lava in the lake of fire was made scientifically. Professor F. G.

Perret came from his observatory by Vesuvius and Professor E. G. Shepherd from the Geophysical Laboratory of the Carnegie Institution at Washington, to study Kilauea, following the beginning of such observations already established by Professor Jaggar of the Massachusetts Institute of Technology.

They stretched a wire cable 1,500 feet long from wall to wall over the lake of fire. They ran wires through pulleys along this cable and dropped the best instruments they had with them straight down. Some of these were broken before registration could be secured. The last thermometer registered 1850° Fahrenheit, remaining steadily at that point until the thermometer was withdrawn. Later it was again lowered, but, according to Professor Shepherd, "Pele arose in her wrath, grasped the thermometer, flung hot lava on the supporting wires, thereby weakening them, and then with a final jerk broke the thermometer from its supports and swallowed it. Pele seems to like ironware for diet."

The record of from 1800° to 2000° Fahrenheit seems to be the normal heat of the lake of fire, sometimes, of course, rising much higher under special conditions. The scientific observers when speaking of lava heat usually say it is 1850° Fahrenheit.

III

Volcanic Activity

In a little note-book in Hilo is a record which from time to time has been studied and copied frequently by visiting scientists. The missionary mother who put down the facts therein recorded never dreamed of being scientific. She simply kept a record. In 1832 Mrs. Sarah J. Lyman came to Hilo, where her husband founded the Hilo Boys' Boarding School, a school, by the way, after which the great Hampton Institute of Virginia was patterned. On October 3, 1833, she was tossed around in her home in a way somewhat alarming. She opened her little note-book and wrote, "Two earthquakes, one of them heavy."

She had a little curiosity to see how frequently these earthquakes disturbed her home. Thus the record went on from month to month and year to year: "Earthquake, motion up and down," "Heavy shake, stone walls down, cream shaken off the milk," "4 A.M., all the family aroused," "Jar and a noise like distant cannon," "Tremendous shock, brace ourselves to stand up," "Kai-mimiki" (sea shaken by an earthquake), "All motions combined, earth like the sea." At one time the record ran: "Frequent jars, severe, so many I have ceased to count."

Interspersed through this concise and interesting story of earthquakes told in a few word pictures are many references to other volcanic phenomena. "Activity great in Mokuaweoweo. Mountain clear for several days, the smoke is marked, light brilliant at night, snow extensive on both mountains."

The year 1863 has been marked as the volcano year of Hawaiian history. Mr. F. S. Lyman, now living in Hilo, wrote a journal letter, which was quoted in full. He writes as follows about the earthquake:

"March 27–31, 1868. A sudden eruption from Mauna Loa, no forewarning, a spray of red lava thrown high in the air, followed by a great stream of smoke rising up thousands of feet. In Kati we had quite a sprinkling of Pele's hair, peculiar earthquakes—first hard shakes, then a swaying motion, as if the whole island were swaying back and forth and we with it. March 31—From about 10 P.M. to 2 A.M. the shaking was incessant, Thursday, April 2nd. We experienced the most fearful of earthquakes. The earth swayed north, south, cast, west, round and round, up and down, and in every imaginable direction, everything crashing around us, trees thrashing as if torn by a mighty wind, impossible to stand. We had to sit on the ground, bracing with hands and feet, to keep from rolling over."

Mr. H. M. Whitney, editor of the Advertiser, says that "the number of shocks which occurred at Waiohinu from March 29 to April 10 was estimated at upwards of two thousand. The heaviest shock, that of April 2d, destroyed every church and nearly every dwelling in the whole district. This earthquake was felt very sensibly in Honolulu. Following the earthquake came a great tidal wave at Punaluu. It rolled in over the tops of coconut trees, probably sixty feet high at least, driving all floating rubbish inland about a quarter of a mile—taking with it, when it returned to the sea, houses, men, and women and everything movable."

Mr. Lyman wrote: "We could see the shore. All along the seashore from directly below us to Punaluu about three or four miles the sea was boiling and foaming furiously, all red."

Two remarkable eruptions accompanied this earthquake. The lava, starting from the slope of Mauna Loa, sank into some great channel but "burst forth with a heavy roar several miles farther down. The lava stream became a river of fire, flowing rapidly toward and around some farmhouses. The inmates had barely time to escape. The path by which they fled was covered with lava within ten minutes after they passed over it. Animals and even human beings perished. The number of deaths were between eighty and one hundred. This eruption flowed ten miles in two hours, and continued five days, destroying many thousands of acres of good lands." The second remarkable eruption was nearer the crater Kilauea and has been known as "The Great Mud Flow of 1868." It is in the region covered by the Pahala plantation.

Mr. Lyman writes: "In the midst of the great earthquake we saw burst out from the top of the pali about a mile and a half north of us, what we supposed to be an immense river of molten lava (which afterward proved to be red earth), which rushed down in headlong course and across the plain below, apparently bursting from the ground and swallowing up everything in its way-trees, houses, cattle, horses, men, in an instant as it were. It went three miles in not more than three minutes' time and then stopped. After the hard shaking had ceased we went right over to a hill with the children and our natives expecting every moment to be swallowed up by the lava from beneath, for it sounded as if it were surging and washing under our feet all the time. Outside of Punaluu we saw a long black point of lava slowly pushing out to sea. An island about four hundred feet high rose out of the sea at the southpoint. The lava river has extended the shore to this island one mile at least."

Mrs. Lyman wrote: "Jan. 30, 1875. Light exceedingly brilliant. Perpendicular column of smoke over 1,000 feet high on the summit crater spreading out at top like an expanding flower." This august glow was described by members of the "Challenger" expedition as "a globular cloud perpetually reformed by condensation, having a brilliant orange glow at night as if a fire were raging in the distance."

This display from the summit of Mauna Loa continued about eighteen months.

Isabella Bird Bishop, author of "Six Months in the Sandwich Islands," visited this active crater in 1874, and wrote about the crater itself. "Nearly opposite us a fountain of pure yellow fire, unlike the gory gleam of Kilauea, was throwing up its glorious incandescence. The sunset gold was not purer than the living fire. The roar of this surging lava sea was a glorious sound, the roar of an ocean at dispeace mingled with the hollow murmur of surf echoing in sea caves, booming on, rising and falling like the thunder music of windward Hawaii. The area below us was over two miles long and a mile and a half wide with precipitous sides and a broad second shelf about 300 feet below the one we occupied with a fire fountain three-quarters of a mile away. On the way up the mountain there was a fearful internal throbbing and rumbling, rocks and masses of soil were dislodged, the earth reeled, then rocked again with such violence that I felt as if the horse and myself had gone over."

During these months of 1874–1875 there were magnificent exhibitions of clouds reflecting volcanic fires caused by the upburst of lava fountains.

The summit crater of Mauna Loa is about 13,000 feet altitude. Snow has frequently covered the top of the mountain, lying in deep banks around the edge of the crater. The cold has acted quickly upon the lake of fire, congealing a large part of the surface into a hard floor of lava. Gases, steam, and smoke lift this floor and break through it with great violence, escaping from the melted lava in pillars of cloud against which the fires beneath mirror themselves in glorious displays of color. These outbursts were frequently called eruptions. The modern name is more correct. They are "glows," reflecting wonderful fires beneath.

Mrs. Lyman mentions another eruption from the summit of Mauna Loa. "1877. Feb. 14. Eruption seen on the mountain. Ten days extinct then broke out lower down the mountain and reached the sea in a few days, near Kaawaloa, Kealakekua Bay."

Dana says, "The columns of illuminated steam rose with fearful speed to a height of 14,000 to 17,000 feet and then spread out into a vast fiery cloud looking at night as if the heavens were on fire."

After this, there was an underground eruption to the sea marked by a fissure down the mountain side through which clouds of steam and smoke were forced. The lava at last found its place for escape under the sea.

H. Al. Whitney, the editor of the Hawaiian Gazette, was a witness of this submarine eruption. In the issue of Feb. 28, 1877, he wrote: "As the steamer Kilauea came toward the bay, the passengers saw some canoes rowing about over boiling water. The natives reported that about three o'clock in the morning of Feb. 24, they had seen innumerable red, blue, and green lights dancing in the waters. Morning disclosed a new volcano in the sea. The southern shore of the bay has been known as Keei point. The eruption appeared to be in a straight line out from this point. Three boats from the steamer went out, cruising over the most active part of the boiling waters, appearing as if passing over rapids. Blocks of lava two feet across were thrown up from beneath, striking the boats and jarring them. The lava was quite soft and no harm was done. Six stones hit the boat in one minute. Several hundred pieces of these stones were floating on the sea at one time. Nearly all the pieces on reaching the surface were red hot, emitting steam and gas strongly sulphurous. Several were taken into the boats, perfectly incandescent and so molten in the interior that the lava could be stirred with a stick, the water having penetrated only about an inch. When these stones cooled and became water soaked they sank rapidly. The specimens taken from the water were of the a-a variety and very light. Probably only the lightest came to the surface. Some of the lava consisted of Pele's hair, red hot, yet preserving its peculiar characteristics."

Mrs. Lyman has the record of a terrible tidal wave which struck Hilo harbor in May of that same year: "1877, May 10. A heavy tidal wave at 5 A.M., destroying 34 houses on the Waiakea side of the harbor, also the bridge and twelve houses between Waialama and Aiko's old store. One hundred and sixty people homeless, some bruised, bones broken, five dead. Wave was thirteen and a half feet above high water mark at Waiakea, swept inland forty rods, accurate measurement." Following this on May 31, came the record "severe shake, things thrown down."

Dana says: "A destructive earthquake wave was felt at the Hawaiian Islands on May 10, 1877, which rose at Hilo to a height of 36 feet. But it was of South American origin, where there were heavy earth-shocks, and not of Hawaiian."

One of the eruptions from Mokuaweoweo tried to take possession of a river-bed, but the waters chilled one side of the lava and built it into a wall. On one side was flowing fire and on the other the swift rapids of a river. The antagonistic elements sought the sea side by side.

A native account of Kilauea in "Ka Hae Hawaii (The Hawaiian Flag)" was published in Honolulu in March, 1859. In it is a very interesting native account of eruptions on the island Hawaii. The sketch is in the quaint Hawaiian tongue and is valuable throughout, but only a few extracts from the translation can be used at present. The story as told by the Hawaiian runs as follows:

"In the very ancient time Mauna Kea threw out vast Pele fires, but long ago these eruptions have been imprisoned. The earth has covered them in on all sides and the abundant soil, large trees, and green things of many kinds are multiplying. But not so Mauna Loa and Hualalai, other mountains of this island Hawaii. Pele fires have burst forth from them even up to recent times.

"Mauna Loa is the greatest of all the mountains, opening doors for the Pele fires from all its sides. Kilauea and Mokuaweoweo are the very wonderful Pele pits (craters) discharging fire from the very depths of the mountains.

"In the year 1822, or 1823 perhaps, there was an eruption from Kilauea pouring down into the Kau district very close to the Puna line. From the depths of Kilauea was this bursting forth. The a-a (broken lava) of this eruption in its journey to the sea spread about eight miles. In the year 1832 the pit of Kilauea was full of burning a-a. It broke into some ancient tunnel connected with Kilauea and flowed away. The place where the a-a reached the sea is not known. It is supposed to have gone into the sea underground.

"In the year 1840, the people of Puna and Hilo districts saw a great fire inland. They thought that the forest wilderness was burning. That day was the Sabbath. The people assembled together and looked toward the place where the fire was very great and the air was heavy with smoke. Then they saw that this was not an ordinary forest fire but a Pele (an eruption). They could not see any a-a breaking out on the mountain, and therefore were greatly afraid that it was very near and would destroy their lands. Volumes of smoke rolled, curling upward, while the strong steam burst forth with reports like the firing of cannon. On the 4th day of June that eruption poured down into the sea. Narrow was the flow in steep places and spread out widely in others. When it came to the sea mighty was the stormy rage and the boiling of the sea, the steam rising in clouds to the sky. There were built up on the beach two hills of black sand, about 400 feet in height. Only on the side from which the wind blew could any one come near. On the other side the smoke was very strong, offensive and sickening like a volcano. Then there were burning ashes destroying every green thing for many miles. The lands of the people of Nanawale were quickly made a desolate wilderness by the heat and the overflowing lava. Some animals were caught by the lava and burned to death. None of the people were destroyed. They escaped with poverty."

A curious and interesting statement is made by the Hawaiian fishermen of Waikiki concerning a peculiar disturbance of the sea simultaneous with all seasons of volcanic agitation. One of the older and more intelligent fishermen says that from his boyhood he has known a pushing up and down, backward and forward, of the waters every time that Mauna Loa has shown activity in either of its great craters. Fishnets are so tossed about that it is almost impossible to retain any fish in them. Hooks are so rapidly moved by the commotion in the waters that fishing with hook and line is not very successful.

The Hawaiians call the ocean at such times kai-mimiki (the rushing sea). Mimiki is defined as a meeting of a returning wave with another advancing, and is sometimes used to express the confusion of advancing and returning tidal waves. Sometimes mimiki is used to denote the choppy waters which follow a storm. The inherent idea of the word seems to be quick, independent action of waves, bringing them into conflict with each other and destroying the quiet, regular motion.

IV

Changes in Kilauea Crater

There have been two entirely distinct modifications in Kilauea. One belongs to the centuries and the mountain which the crater has been trying to build. The other relates to the fire-pit and the fire-lake therein.

Kilauea is a mountain a little over 4,000 feet in altitude, closely connected with Mauna Loa, which is about 13,000 feet in altitude. It has been stated that there is some connection which affects the action of two lakes of lava in the two craters.

Kilauea is a great bowl sunken in a plain which seems level but which slopes decidedly toward the large mountain on the one side and the ocean on the other. Above the present fire-pit rise great plateaus and a summit 500 feet above the edges of the present crater, and about one mile east of it. This elevation shows that at one time the lake of fire had its real crater rim extending far back of the site of the Volcano Hotel and very much higher than at present, and that great floods of lava were poured out over the surrounding country at a height impossible for the new crater to attain. After these eruptions the fire-pit sank away, leaving great precipitous walls and wide cracks out of which even now pour clouds of steam of such intense heat and such powerful sulphur fumes that animals falling in are killed instantly.

There are several terraces showing how the precipices, cracks, and plateaus followed each other step by step down to the bed of Kilauea itself. There are hints of these changes in the traditions of the Hawaiians, but it is impossible to know exactly what is meant. Rev. William Ellis, author of "Polynesian Researches," and a deputation of the American missionaries studying the opportunities for missionary labor, while making a tour around Hawaii in 1823, visited Kilauea and wrote the following description of the volcano. In this report, afterward incorporated in "Polynesian Researches" as Volume Iv, the following account is given of ancient Kilauea. "We asked the natives with us to tell us what they knew of the history of this volcano. From them we learned that it had been burning from time immemorial, or to use their own words 'mai ka po mai' (from chaos until now) and had inundated some part of the country during the reign of every king that had governed Hawaii. In earlier ages it used to boil up, overflow its banks, and inundate the adjacent country; but for many kings' reigns past it had kept below the level of the surrounding plain, continually extending its surface and increasing its depth, and occasionally throwing up with violent explosions huge rocks and red hot stones. These eruptions, they said, were always accompanied by dreadful earthquakes, loud claps of thunder and vivid and quick succeeding lightning. No great explosion, they added, had taken place since the days of Keoua (a part of whose army was destroyed by a shower of ashes and foul gases in 1790), but many places near the sea had since been overflowed, on which occasions Pele went by a road underground from her house in the crater to the shore."

Concerning Pele the natives said, "Kirauea had been burning ever since the islands had emerged from night, but it was not inhabited till after the 'Tai a ka Hina rii,' the sea or deluge of Hina the chief." Shortly, after this flood they say the present volcanic family carne from Tahiti, meaning some foreign country, to Hawaii.

When the crater was "boiling up, overflowing its banks, and inundating the adjacent territory," as the natives said, it poured out lava which became solid rock. As it went westward, the character of its overflow changed, becoming explosive, hurling out cinders and ashes instead of boiling lava, so that all the land, especially toward the south and west, is covered with volcanic ash. For more than a hundred years there has been no uplift of lava or ashes over the outside crater rim.

During this century there has been no marked change in the great edge of the bowl, but the interior has been kaleidoscopic. The bowl is flat-bottomed with a surface creased and cracked and rough, with twisted piles of dead lava. In innumerable spots any cool morning welcomes rising clouds of steam and in the western part is the Lua-Pele, a pit filled with living fire. This outer crater is about three and a half miles across.

A hundred years ago the floor of this crater was the scene of continual activity. Around the entire rim was a black ledge or balcony against which fountains of lava hurled their repeated drops, falling on the black ledge. Now, the fire-pit is but a little over a quarter of a mile in diameter, and yet it has the same form of black ledge which had been built up in the great crater so many years before.

When first visited by the missionaries, there were many hilly islands, fountain cones, and hissing blowholes. Later, the great floor began to cool and lakes appeared in different sections.

In 1890, when the writer first saw the home of the fire-goddess, there were three lakes through which eruptive gases burst with explosions like the continual rattle of artillery, and there were two great rivers of lava flowing across the wide, black floor of the vast crater. Now there is only one lake of fire. Ka Lua Pele, the "Pit of Pele," is at present on a small scale what the crater of Kilauea was in its magnitude in 1823 and for many years thereafter.

The brief mention of shifting fires, flowing rivers, raging lakes, deep pits, falling walls, and frozen uneven lava surfaces must suffice to make evident the stupendous forces of nature which have terrified the Hawaiians for centuries and have made them build up legends in and around these terrors and have created the demand for a special fire-goddess to take rank with the other gods worshipped.

V

Foundation of the Observatory

Excerpts from the Report of the Hawaiian Volcano observatory Jan.–Mch., 1912. —Published by the Society of Arts of the Massachusetts Institute of Technology, Boston.

The Hawaiian Volcano Observatory, now in operation for five years from July 1, 1912, under the direction of the Department of Geology of the Massachusetts Institute of Technology, is the result and culmination of a succession of investigations, constructions, appointments, and expeditions, mostly under that institution, which began in 1898 with the building of a small geodetic observatory in Boston. The work has been concerned with geodesy, astronomy, magnetism, and geology, and has been partly Under the direction of officers of the Department of Civil Engineering and partly under professors of geology. The result of this activity that had the most direct bearing on the establishment of the volcano observatory was its influence on the trustees of the Whitney estates, who, on July 1, 1900 gave to the Institute the sum of twenty-five thousand dollars ($25,000) as a memorial of Edward and Caroline Rogers Whitney of Boston, for the conduct of research or teaching in geophysics to include investigations in seismology, conducted with a view to the protection of human life and property, present preference being that some investigations in geophysics be undertaken in Hawaii.

The purpose of the science of geophysics is to investigate all the physical and chemical processes going on in the earth. Recent disasters such as Messina and San Francisco have shown how defective, for humane and practical purposes, our knowledge of these processes is. Before the intervention of the Whitney trustees, it had been the desire of the Institute to secure a volcanic site in order to observe the local activities of a particular volcano, as well as the waves which pass through the earth from distant earthquakes. Professor Jaggar had, for sometime past, been investigating and considering this subject.

After mature deliberation Professor Jaggar concluded that Kilauea affords the best point for the location of the proposed observatory among those places in the world which have come to his knowledge, for the following reasons:

"1. At other volcanoes the eruptions are more explosive and an observatory located close enough to the centre of activity is in some danger. Kilauea, while displaying great and varied activity, is relatively safe.

"2. Other volcanoes are more or less connected in chains, making many stations necessary in order to determine the relations of the different craters to each other. Kilauea and Mauna Loa form an isolated centre of activity over 2,000 miles from the nearest active vent, so that the phenomena of these two vents can be recorded without complications occasioned by other nearby centres.

"3. Kilauea is very accessible. The near-by harbor at Hilo is only thirty-one miles distant; it may be reached by railroad and a good driveway, and Honolulu, a centre of traffic and science, is easily reached in a day.

"4. The Central Pacific position is unique, and is of advantage for recording distant earthquakes through the uninterrupted sea floor which lies between Hawaii and many earthquake places such as South America, Mexico, and Japan. For expeditions in case of disaster or otherwise, a relatively short route is assured, with abundant means of transportation to Pacific and East Indian ports. For the study of the deep sea floor, Hawaii is obviously favorable.

"5. The climate is uniform and the air clear for astronomical work.

"6. There are frequent small earthquakes, which are of great interest for technical reasons.

"7. The remarkable distribution of both hot and cold underground waters in Hawaii needs careful study, and this has an important bearing on agriculture as well as upon science.

"8. The territory is American, and these volcanoes are famous in the history of science for their remarkably liquid lavas and nearly continuous activity."

Professor Jaggar consequently advised those interested:

"1. To erect buildings on the brink of the Volcano of Kilauea, in which to house the instruments, library, and offices for working up and tabulating the statistics, records, and information obtained.

"2. To set apart a room for a local museum, to exhibit to visitors instruments, plans, diagrams, maps, and photographs. This will be of value in exciting interest with a view to securing an endowment.

"3. To welcome advanced students from either the Institute or other institutions for special work in the laboratory.

"4. To erect subordinate instrument stations, with self-recording instruments, and to employ voluntary observers, at various points hereafter to be determined. It is hoped that eventually some work will be done by the staff of the observatory in the study of tides, soundings, earthquake waves, and the movements of the coast line of the island.

"5. To send expeditions to other volcanic and earthquake belts for comparative studies,

"6. To carry on research, as may seem expedient, in terrestrial gravitation, magnetism, and variation of latitude.

"7. To make a geological survey of the Island of Hawaii. It is hoped that this will lead to a thorough survey of the whole territory by the United States Geological Survey."

He added that the main object of all the work should be humanitarian—earthquake prediction and methods of protecting life and property on the basis of sound scientific achievement.

"Results obtained in connection with all subjects of investigation should be promptly published in the form of bulletins and memoirs."

In pursuit of these ideas, Professor Jaggar proceeded to enlist support from the Chamber of Commerce and the leading citizens of Honolulu. A generous response came from a number of organizations, including the Bishop Museum and individuals.

The total amount promised was $3,450 per year for a period of five years. This sum was not sufficient to do the work satisfactorily and the development of the plan was halted in consequence.

—The subscription of the Bishop Museum was made upon the

condition that the Institute shall furnish the trustees without expense except for transportation, samples of all museum specimens collected, properly described, also copies of all published maps, surveys, and literature made by the Institute in connection with Hawaiian interests.—

In the course of a journey to Japan Mr. Jaggar visited the volcano Kilauea in Hawaii twice, in March and in July, 1909. Professor Daly spent the summer in the Hawaiian Islands, making careful study of Kilauea and the result of his work has since been published in vol. 47, no. 3, of the Proceedings of the American Academy of Arts and Sciences under the title, "The Nature of Volcanic Action." Both of these expeditions were at private expense.

In 1910 the first available income of the Whitney fund was used in the construction of special resistance thermometers made by Leeds and Northrup at Baltimore under the direction of Drs. A. L. Day and E. S. Shepherd of the Geophysical Laboratory of the Carnegie Institution of Washington. Dr. Day, director of this laboratory, in correspondence with Professors Daly and Jaggar during the winter of 1909–10 agreed to send Dr. Shepherd to Kilauea and provide travelling expenses if the Institute of Technology would provide instruments and living expenses during a stay at the Volcano House devoted to measurement of the temperature of liquid lava. Dr. Shepherd is a chemist and a specialist in pyrometric work. With the aid of Institute engineers a cableway was designed for spanning the inner pit of Halemaumau wherewith by a wire trolley system pyrometric apparatus might be lowered into the lava.

During 1909 and 1910 three seismographs, in addition to the Bosch-Omori instruments already obtained with Whitney funds, were constructed for the Institute in Tokyo under Dr. Omori's direction, and shipped to Honolulu.

For two years in succession, 1910 and 1911, it was impossible for any of the professors of geology at the Institute to go to Hawaii, so arrangements were made with Mr. F. A. Perret of Springfield, Mass., and Naples, Italy, to take Professor Jaggar's place in an expedition to Kilauea for the measurement of temperatures as agreed with the Carnegie Geophysical Laboratory. The sum of $2,100 from the Whitney and other geological research funds of the Institute was expended on this expedition. The Institute is indebted to the Carnegie Geophysical Laboratory for co-operation and for the thermo-element which was used in the final test, and to the Volcanic Research Society of Springfield, Mass., for the loan of the services of Mr. Perret, his salary being continued by that society during his Hawaiian journey. Mr. Perret built a wooden camp on the edge of the pit Halemaumau which he called the Technology Station and where he lived.

It will appear from the foregoing that the work bearing on a proposed volcano observatory in Hawaii up to 1912 was instituted and carried forward by the Massachusetts Institute of Technology. That institution was materially aided in the conduct of this work by voluntary subscription among citizens of Honolulu.

Some $6,100, in addition to salaries, was spent by the Institute of Technology for its officers for work in Hawaii prior to 1912, and after Mr. Perret's departure in November, 1911, an appropriation of $1,700 for Professor Jaggar's work in Hawaii in the winter of 1912 was made from Technology funds.

The subscription fund provided for in Honolulu in 1909 was revived on October 5, 1911, at a luncheon at the University Club, given for the organization of a Hawaiian Volcano Research Association.

The net result of this meeting was to establish an association in Honolulu for the subscription of money to volcano research. The committee representative of this association determined to name the organization "Hawaiian Volcano Research Association." Funds for the running expense of an observatory on Hawaii to the amount of $5,000 annually for five years from January 1, 1912, exclusive of the funds furnished by the Massachusetts Institute of Technology were subscribed, the full amount in the event of failure on the part of individual subscribers being guaranteed by Mr. Clarence H. Cooke, treasurer, through the generosity of Mr. Cooke and his associates of the estate of C. M. Cooke, Ltd.

The Institute was prepared to co-operate with the Hawaiian Volcano Research Association by becoming its largest subscriber for the five years, through the income of the Whitney fund and the current payment to its Seismological fund.

On January 19 a subscription was started in the town of Hilo to provide funds wherewith to build a laboratory near the Volcano House for the use of the representative of the Massachusetts Institute of Technology engaged in volcanic research. This proposal met a most hearty response and within a few days $1,785 was subscribed.

The land for the Observatory, a tract of about three acres, was obtained on a sub-lease for fifteen years to October 1, 1927, from the Volcano House Company with the consent of the trustees of the Bishop

Estate, the owners of the land. This tract is on the edge of the cliff directly opposite the grounds of the Volcano House on the south side of the Puna-Kau road. The observatory is built of Oregon pine and is equipped with two laboratories, the director's room, photographic dark room, and storeroom on the main floor. A veranda extending along two sides commands extensive views of the three volcanoes, Kilauea, Mauna Loa, and Mauna Kea. In front there is a concrete post for geodetic and photographic experiments. The furniture includes large cases of drawers, for storage of specimens, maps, or photographs, and there are work and drafting tables.

The Whitney Laboratory of Seismology, eighteen feet square, is a basement room of concrete floored on the solid ledge of basalt. This is the rock of the upper-most layer of the cliff which here borders the greater crater of Kilauea. The cellar was dug through 5½ feet of ash and pumice which make the surface soil. The piers for seismographs were designed for a set of instruments built in Tokyo in 1910 under the direction of Professor Omori and purchased with the income of the Whitney fund.

On January 24,1912, Mr. F. B. Dodge of Honolulu arrived at the volcano to become assistant to the director and during the ensuing weeks arrangements were completed and trigonometric stations installed whereby a daily survey of the active lava pool could be made.

The Territorial Government loaned the services of a part of the prison gang which does the road work for the Territory of Hawaii, to clear the land, dig the cellar, and build the roadway of the Observatory.

An additional hut constructed wholly without iron for possible magnetic work was built on the verge of Halemaumau for direct instrumental observations of the lava, under shelter.

The fundamental idea expressed at the time of the formation of the Hawaiian Volcano Research Association was to the effect that the crater observations should be continuous and permanent. From the point of view of the educator, however, there is another equally vital work to be accomplished by such an experiment station as the Hawaiian Volcano Observatory, namely, provision for scientific hospitality. The study of geophysics and geochemistry in the field is so extensive and inclusive a department of science that no resident staff could hope to cover the whole field without large expense and a very large working force. Moreover the spirit of generous exchange of opportunity and of ideas in science, with a liberal welcome to serious students of all schools, is modern and novel, and should promote the most rapid progress. Accordingly it is proposed in the Hawaiian Observatory to combine two objects, record of facts of volcanology and seismology by the permanent staff, and surveys in the field of special topics by expert specialists invited to come from other institutions.

Appendix

Polynesian Language

A few words should be added on the peculiar genius and structure of the Polynesian language in general and of the Hawaiian dialect in particular.

It is the law of all Polynesian languages that every word and syllable must end in a vowel, so that no two consonants are ever heard without a vowel sound between them.

Most of the radical words are dissyllables, and the accent is generally on the penult. The Polynesian ear is as nice in marking the slightest variations in vowel sound as it is dull in distinguishing consonants.

The vocabulary of the Hawaiian is probably richer than that of most other Polynesian tongues. Its child-like and primitive character is shown by the absence of abstract words and general terms.

As has been well observed by M. Gaussin, there are three classes of words, corresponding to as many different stages of language: first, those that express sensations; second, images; third, abstract ideas.

Not only are names wanting for the more general abstractions, such as space, nature, fate, etc., but there are very few generic terms. For example there is no generic term for animal, expressing the whole class of living creatures or for insects or for colors. At the same time it abounds in specific names and in nice distinctions.

So in the Hawaiian everything that relates to their everyday life or to the natural objects with which they are conversant is expressed with a vivacity, a minuteness and nicety of coloring which cannot be reproduced in a foreign tongue. Thus the Hawaiian was very rich in terms for every variety of cloud. It has names for every species of plant on the mountains or fish in the sea, and is peculiarly copious in terms relating to the ocean, the surf and waves.

For whatever belonged to their religions, their handicrafts or their amusements, their vocabulary was most copious and minute. Almost every stick in a native house had its appropriate name. Hence it abounds in synonyms which are such only in appearance, *i.e.*, "to be broken" as a stick is 'haki,' as a string is 'moku,' as a dish 'naha,' as a wall 'hina.'

Besides the language of every-day life, there was a style appropriate to oratory and another to religion and poetry.

The above-mentioned characteristics make it a pictorial and expressive language. It still has the freshness of childhood. Its words are pictures rather than colorless and abstract symbols of ideas, and are redolent of the mountain, the forest and the surf.

However it has been and is successfully used to express the abstractions of mathematics, of English law, and of theology."

"The Hawaiian is but a dialect of the great Polynesian language, which is spoken with extraordinary uniformity over all the numerous islands of the Pacific Ocean between New Zealand and Hawaii. Again, the Polynesian language is but one member-of that wide-spread family of languages, known as the Malayo-Polynesian or Oceanic family, which extends from Madagascar to the Hawaiian Islands and from New Zealand to Formosa. The Hawaiian dialect is peculiarly interesting to the philologist from its isolated position, being the most remote of the family from its primeval seat in Southeastern Asia, and leading the van with the Malagasy in the rear. We believe the Hawaiian to be the most copious and expressive, as well as the richest in native traditional history and poetry. Dr. Reinhold Forster, the celebrated naturalist of Captain Cook's second voyage, drew up a table containing 47 words taken from 11 Oceanic dialects and the corresponding terms in Malay, Mexican, Peruvian and Chilian. From this table he inferred that the Polynesian languages afford many analogies with the Malay while they present no point of contact with the American."

Baron William von Humboldt, the distinguished statesman and scholar, showed that the Tagala, the leading language of the Philippine Islands, is by far the richest and most perfect of these languages. "It possesses," he says, "all the forms collectively of which particular ones are found singly in other dialects; and it has preserved them all with very trifling exceptions unbroken and in entire harmony and symmetry."

The languages of the Oceanic region have been divided into six great groups; i.e., the Polynesian; the Micronesian; the Melanesian or Papuan; the Australian; the Malaysian; the Malagasy. Many examples might be given if they were needed to illustrate the connection of these languages. The Polynesian is an ancient and primitive member of the Malay family. The New Zealand dialect is the most primitive and entire in its forms. The Hawaiians, Marquesans and Tahitians form a closely related group by themselves. For example, the Marquesan converts are using Hawaiian books and the people of the Austral Islands read the Tahitian Bible."

The above was written by W. D. Alexander in Honolulu in 1865, author of the "History of the Hawaiian Islands" as preface to Andrew's Dictionary.

A Note About the Author

W.D. Westervelt (1849–1939) was an American minister, historian, and folklorist specializing in Hawaiian mythology. Born in Oberlin, Ohio, he obtained his B.A. from Oberlin College before completing his B.D. from Oberlin Theological Seminary in 1874. In 1899, after serving as a pastor in Ohio and Colorado, Westervelt settled in Hawaii, where he married Caroline Dickinson Castle. A member of the Hawaiian Historical Society, he served as secretary, treasurer, and president, gaining a reputation as a leading scholar of Hawaiian folklore. Throughout his career, he wrote numerous articles and several anthologies on Hawaiian myths and legends, which continue to be recognized as some of the most reliable sources on the subject written in English.

A Note from the Publisher

Spanning many genres, from non-fiction essays to literature classics to children's books and lyric poetry, Mint Edition books showcase the master works of our time in a modern new package. The text is freshly typeset, is clean and easy to read, and features a new note about the author in each volume. Many books also include exclusive new introductory material. Every book boasts a striking new cover, which makes it as appropriate for collecting as it is for gift giving. Mint Edition books are only printed when a reader orders them, so natural resources are not wasted. We're proud that our books are never manufactured in excess and exist only in the exact quantity they need to be read and enjoyed.

bookfinity™

Discover more of your favorite classics with Bookfinity™.

- Track your reading with custom book lists.
- Get great book recommendations for your personalized Reader Type.
- Add reviews for your favorite books.
- AND MUCH MORE!

Visit **bookfinity.com** and take the fun Reader Type quiz to get started.

Enjoy our classic and modern companion pairings!

Classic & Modern